"I celebrate Diane's commitment to teaching higher truths. She is a light that illuminates my life."

"Diane is a masterful, heart-centered teacher of miracle living. I find her loving wisdom a powerful tool to remember heaven even as I walk the earth."

"You may be sure that *Love Always Answers* when Diane speaks or writes. I know of no one who better demonstrates being the Presence of Love. Sharing her presence in this book becomes an *experience* of *A Course in Miracles*."

"I deeply appreciate Diane's work."

"Diane brings a quality of sincerity and clarity to our collective quest for healing and awakening. She has touched many hearts through her work in Interfaith Fellowship and provides impeccable guidance to students of *A Course in Miracles* everywhere. *Love Always Answers* will be a blessing for anyone who reads it."

"Diane is deeply devoted to her spiritual awakening. Her willingness to listen for and follow Love's inner urgings and her ability to share her process with others are a beautiful gift to us all."

"Diane's book should be *must* reading for all those in the field, or on the path, of healing. Her style is intimate, informative, and highly spiritual. The reader will be impressed with her insight and inspired by her passion and love for humanity. I highly recommend *Love Always Answers* to be part of the basic library of everyone seeking spiritual answers and meaning to the problems of life."

LOVE ALWAYS ANSWERS

to Pat
with love &
blessings —
Diane Berke

LOVE ALWAYS ANSWERS

WALKING THE PATH OF
"Miracles"

DIANE BERKE

CROSSROAD · NEW YORK

1994

The Crossroad Publishing Company
370 Lexington Avenue, New York, NY 10017

Library of Congress Cataloging-in-Publication Data
Berke, Diane.
    Love always answers : walking the path of "Miracles" / by Diane Berke.
      p. cm.
    Includes bibliographical references.
    ISBN 0-8245-1432-7
    1. Course in miracles. 2. Spiritual life. I. Title.
BP605.C68B47   1994
299'.93—dc20
                                  94-27544
                                     CIP

To the many teachers
who have illumined and guided
my journey
and to the one
Teacher of Love
who speaks through them all

Contents

Acknowledgments

There are so many to whom I am deeply indebted and grateful on my journey and in the "coming-into-being" of this book. I offer my heartfelt appreciation and love to:

- The members of Interfaith Fellowship and readers of *On Course* magazine, for their ongoing feedback, encouragement, and love.

- Dr. Kenneth Wapnick, for his example, his dedication, and the incredible clarity, depth, and purity of his teaching. Although there are interpretations in this book with which he would disagree, my basic understanding of the Course is very much filtered through Ken's teaching. My debt and gratitude to him are profound. I have tried to credit him specifically throughout this book wherever I recognized to do so. However, if I have inadvertently failed to do so at times, I sincerely regret any such oversights.

- Michael Leach of Crossroad Publishing Company, for his persistence, unflagging enthusiasm, and amazing blend of flexibility and focus at every stage of this project. I cannot imagine a more supportive or delightful publisher to work with.

- My extended "spiritual family" — I must trust that you know who you are, for you are, blessedly, too many to mention by name. You have loved, encouraged, and walked beside me at every step of this journey home we share.

- My grandfather, whose quiet example of what it meant to be a truly religious and loving human being started me on the path to a God-infused life.

- My mother, for encouraging me to learn, and for being willing to grow and heal with me again and again.

- Rabbi Joseph Gelberman, for his abiding friendship and love, for the inclusiveness of his spirit and heart, and for being my teacher of joy.

- Donna Cary, my sister in spirit, whose voice and message, love and presence, never fail to open my heart and cause me to remember.

- Rudy, Cinnamon, Pepper, Skunk, Mussy, and Serica — the four-legged teachers of love who have shared and graced my life and have been a source of so much love and laughter, silliness and solace along the way.

- Eric Butterworth, minister of Unity of New York. The integrity and intelligence of his teaching and the example and power of his unswerving dedication to truth have been guiding stars on my journey and were my inspiration to enter ministry.

- And finally, Jon Mundy, my partner in Interfaith Fellowship and *On Course*. Without his presence in my life and his loving encouragement over the years, this book would never have been written.

Referencing Key for Quotations from
A Course in Miracles

Passages quoted from *A Course in Miracles* are referenced in the following standard way:

> T: Text
> W: Workbook
> M: Manual for Teachers
> C: Clarification of Terms
> SOP: The Song of Prayer

(Note: *The Song of Prayer* is a pamphlet received after the Course through the same process of inner dictation. It contains a further elaboration of the Course's teachings on prayer, forgiveness, and healing.)

Each passage cited contains two references. The first refers to the first edition of the Course, published in 1976. The second refers to the second edition, published in 1992.

Examples:

— T. p. 200; T-12.I.3:1-4

T. p. 200 — Text (1st edition), page 200

T-12 — Text (2nd edition), Chapter 12

I — Subsection I of the chapter

3 — Paragraph 3 of the subsection

1–4 — Sentences 1 through 4 of the paragraph

— W. p. 93; W-Pt.I.r.I.57.3

W. p. 93 — Workbook (1st edition), page 93

W-Pt.I.r.I — Workbook (2nd edition), Part I, Review I

57 — Lesson 57

3 — Paragraph 3 of the lesson

— M. p. 3; M-1.4:2

M. p. 3 — Manual for Teachers (1st edition), page 3

M-1 — Manual for Teachers (2nd edition), Question 1

4 — Paragraph 4 of Question 1

2 — Sentence 2 of Paragraph 4

— M. p. 77; C-2.6:2-13

M. p. 77 — Manual for Teachers (1st edition), page 77

C-2 — Clarification of Terms (2nd edition), Section 2 (Note: The Clarification of Terms is the last part of the Manual for Teachers)

6 — Paragraph 6 of Section 2

2-13 — Sentences 2 through 13 of Paragraph 6

— SOP. p. 11; SOP-2.I.8:1

SOP. p. 11 — The Song of Prayer (1st edition), page 11

SOP-2 — The Song of Prayer (2nd edition), Section 2

I — Subsection I of Section 2

8 — Paragraph 8 of Subsection I

1 — Sentence 1 of Paragraph 8

All quotations from the Course and the Song of Prayer contained in this book are reprinted with permission of The Foundation for Inner Peace. The ideas and viewpoint presented here reflect the understanding, interpretation, and experience of the author and do not necessarily express the views of those who hold the copyright on the Course.

Preface

The inspiration or impetus to undertake the spiritual journey comes in many different ways. Joseph Goldstein and Jack Kornfield, teachers of Insight Meditation, write in *Seeking the Heart of Wisdom:*

> *"For some of us, this [inspiration] will come as a sense of the great possibility of living in an awake and free way. Others of us are brought to practice as a way to come to terms with the power of suffering in our life. Some are inspired to seek understanding through a practice of discovery and inquiry, while some intuitively sense a connection with the divine or are inspired to practice as a way to open the heart more fully. Whatever brings us to spiritual practice can become a flame in our heart that guides and protects us and brings us to true understanding."*
>
> — Joseph Goldstein and Jack Kornfield,
> *Seeking the Heart of Wisdom*, p. 4

As I reflect on my own life and searching, it is clear that the strongest force in my coming to this journey was the need to face and come to terms with the experience of suffering — in my own life, in the lives of people I cared about, in the world around me. Perhaps that is why I have been so drawn, in addition to the teachings of my chosen path, to the teachings of the Buddha as well. For it is there — with the experience of suffering in this world — that his teachings begin.

A Course in Miracles states,

> *"Tolerance for pain may be high, but it is not without limit. Eventually everyone begins to recognize, however dimly, that there must*

*be a better way. As this recognition becomes more firmly established, it
becomes a turning-point."*

$\qquad\qquad\qquad\qquad\qquad\qquad$ — T. p. 18; T-2.III.3:5–7

It was precisely out of such a moment of recognition that the Course
itself was born.

The Story of the Course

Helen Shucman, who received the Course through a process of
inner dictation, described its origins in this way:

*"A Course in Miracles began with the sudden decision of two peo-
ple to join in a common goal. Their names were Helen Shucman
and William Thetford, Professors of Medical Psychology at Columbia
University's College of Physicians and Surgeons in New York City.
They were anything but spiritual. Their relationship with each other
was difficult and often strained, and they were concerned with personal and professional acceptance and status. In general, they had
considerable investment in the values of the world. Their lives were
hardly in accord with anything that the Course advocates."*

$\qquad\qquad\qquad\qquad\qquad\qquad$ — Preface: How It Came, p. vii

One day in 1965, while on their way to the type of professional
meeting that is generally rife with academic and political backbiting
and one-upmanship, Bill uncharacteristically exclaimed that he was
"tired of the angry and aggressive feelings" such attitudes reflected and
"concluded that 'there must be another way'" (Preface, p. vii). Helen,
equally uncharacteristically, *"as if on cue,...agreed to help him find it"*
(Preface, p. vii).

Three months later, following an intense period of highly sym-
bolic dreams and images, Helen began to experience an inner Voice
requesting that she take notes. With Bill's ongoing encouragement and
emotional support she complied — although the process was a source
of considerable anxiety and psychological discomfort to her initially,
and intermittently throughout. Over a period of seven years, *A Course
in Miracles* was recorded through this process of inner dictation.

While the Course seemed to be in direct answer to Helen and Bill's request for another, better, way of relating to each other, it was clear that the principles and teachings it contained were *universal* in their scope and applicability and not intended solely for the two of them. The Course was first published in 1976. A second edition, with a more detailed system for referencing the material, was completed and published in 1992.

(Those interested in a detailed account of the origins of the Course are encouraged to read *Absence from Felicity*, by Kenneth Wapnick, or *Journey without Distance*, by Robert Skutch.)

The Course as a Path of Healing and Awakening

The Course is not a new religion, although it presents and is based upon a comprehensive, consistent, and profound theological and metaphysical system of thought. It claims to have no corner on the truth. Rather it indicates that it is only one path among many thousands (M. p. 3; M-1.4:2). Moreover, it states,

"Theological considerations as such are necessarily controversial, since they depend on belief and can therefore be accepted or rejected. A universal theology is impossible, but a universal experience is not only possible but necessary. It is this experience toward which the course is directed."
— M. p. 73; C-Intro.2:4–6

"This is not a course in philosophical speculation. . . . It is concerned only with Atonement, or the correction of perception. The means of the Atonement is forgiveness."
— M. p. 73; C-Intro.1:1–3

The emphasis of the Course is very much on experience — the experience of healing our suffering at its source — which according to the Course is our belief in separation and feeling of estrangement from God and our true Self — through the spiritual practice of *forgiveness* in our relationships.

The Course has been described — accurately, I believe — as a system of spiritual psychotherapy. For myself, I think of it as a spiritual path of healing and awakening, whose core practices are forgiveness and developing a relationship with our Inner Teacher, Whom the Course calls the Holy Spirit. It is the Holy Spirit Who teaches us the true meaning of forgiveness, guides us through it, and directs the course of our healing.

The Voice of the Course

The "author" of the Course — the first-person Voice of the Course — is Jesus. In the Course he refers to himself as our *"elder brother"* (T. p. 5; T-1.II.3, 4) — one who completed and fully accomplished the learning process we all must undertake. He is the symbol for us of *egolessness*, and thus of pure Love. In the Course he is referred to also as *"the manifestation of the Holy Spirit"* (M. p. 85; C-6.1:1), because even while in this world he learned to *"hear only that Voice and no other"* (T. p. 69; T-5.II.3:9, 11).

That Voice — the Voice for God, the Voice of Love — calls to us from beyond space and time, yet speaks to us from nearer than our own hearts and breathing. It calls us to remember and return. Learning to listen to and trust that Voice as our guide and teacher is, at the heart, what our journey of healing is all about. Our goal is basically, as St. Paul expressed it, to learn to *"let the mind be in us that was in Christ Jesus."*

The Purpose of this Book

This book is not intended to be a comprehensive overview or presentation of the teachings of the Course. We will look in only the most cursory way, for example, at the metaphysics of the Course, and those interested in understanding that aspect of the Course in depth are referred to the extensive writings and teachings of Dr. Kenneth Wapnick of the Foundation for "A Course in Miracles."

This book is offered, rather, as a simple sharing from my heart, to give readers new to the Course some feeling for what this path of healing is like, and readers already working with the Course some feeling of companionship on the journey.

Most of the chapters in this book were first published between 1992 and January 1994 as articles for *On Course,* a biweekly inspirational magazine that I copublish and edit with Jon Mundy. They were chosen to reflect the title and theme of this book, but should be viewed more as a collection of related pieces than as a unified flow or development from beginning to end.

I write primarily as a way of deepening my own study and learning and share these writings only in the hope that they might be helpful to others on their path. I am a *student* of the Course, not an expert or authority on it. It is my personal path and practice. It is the way of my heart.

I often find when I am writing about a particular topic or theme that life challenges me to confront in a living way whatever I am writing about, to enter into a deeper passage of my own healing. That has turned out to be the case in the process of preparing this manuscript. Two days before the earthquake hit California, it hit my life. There had been tremors in my mind and heart for some time before.

What has been sustaining me and giving me the courage to travel through the darkness toward light, through fear and pain toward love, is the foundation of faith I've developed to this point on my journey. And through this experience, I continue to learn, in an ever deeper way, that Love does answer us — Love always answers.

DIANE BERKE
New York City
February 1994

LOVE ALWAYS ANSWERS

REAL LOVE

There's a love not of this world,
The only Real Love
You'll not find it wherever you search
It's only in the waking up
Wake up, to what you really are
Wake up . . .

You are the very thing you've been searching for,
The very thing you thought you needed more of
Guiltless, sinless Child of God, Love is all you are

There's a love not of this world,
The only Real Love
You'll not find it wherever you search
It's only in the waking up
Wake up, to what you really are
Wake up . . .

Search only for what is false and let it go
Give up the cost of holding on to what you think you know
Listen to the Voice of Love, It's calling you, telling you
Wake up to the only true reality of you

You are a Love not of this world
The only Real Love
You'll not find it wherever you search
It's only in the waking up
Wake up to what you really are
Wake up . . .

This world offers you nothing that you need
You are the extension of all that is and ever will be
When will you believe, when will you come home to Me?
Wake up, wake up and see

A love not of this world
The only Real Love
You'll not find it wherever you search
It's only in the waking up
Wake up, to what you really are
Wake up, to all you've ever been
Wake up ... Wake up ... Wake up ...

— Donna Cary, *Real Love*

Chapter 1

"First Dream of Peace..."

Healing Our Dream of Separation

*"You dwell not here, but in eternity.
You travel but in dreams, while safe at home."*

— T. p. 240; T-13.VII.17:6–7

*"You are at home in God, dreaming of exile
but perfectly capable of awakening to reality.
Is it your decision to do so?"*

— T. p. 169; T-10.I.2:1–2

The journey of healing begins with the need for healing. And our need for healing began, the Course teaches, when we accepted into a tiny part of our mind a thought that the *impossible* had actually occurred.

The Course describes it this way:

*"Into eternity, where all is one,
there crept a tiny, mad idea,
at which the Son of God remembered not
to laugh."*

— T. p. 544; T-27.VIII.6:2

Eternity is Heaven, the oneness and unity of God and His Creation. God is Source, First Cause, Creator. Creation is described as the *extension of being*. There is but one Creation, which the Course calls *Christ*, or the Son of God, which shares all the attributes of God, being the extension of God. God and His Creation are pure spirit, formless, changeless, immortal, and eternal.

Only what God creates is real, and all that is created must share God's own nature. God is only Life, God is only Love, and so reality must be as well. Whatever *appears* otherwise cannot be real, because it cannot be of God.

The "tiny, mad idea" that is the source of all our problems and pain is the idea of separation — the idea that it is possible for a part of God's Creation to wrench itself away, to establish itself as autonomous and opposed to the Will and nature of its Creator. It is the idea that we could be more powerful than God, that we somehow have the power to destroy or change what He created eternal and changeless as Himself.

The Course teaches that this idea is insane and merely laughable if its true absurdity is recognized. Not only could the impossible not occur, the Course teaches, it did not occur. Reality and God and our true Identity and nature remain as They have always been and will forever be.

And yet, the Course describes, when the idea of separation was taken seriously, it is *as if* God's Son fell asleep and dreamed a dream of exile, misery, and death. He dreamed that he was no longer his Father's Son, like his Father in all ways. He dreamed that he was guilty of shattering the wholeness of Heaven and of turning his Father's nature from perfect love to vengeance and wrath. And he dreamed that he must live in terror of punishment and hide himself from his Father's retribution.

He dreamed a world in which to hide — a world unlike Creation in every respect, a world of fragmentation, sorrow, and loss, a world of scarcity and competition and war, a world of sickness and isolation and tears. He dreamed a world where we are born in pain and the only certainty is that we will die. And we search this world, in desperation and futility, for something to fill our longing and emptiness — something to replace the love, the wholeness, the deep sense of home we believe is lost to us forever.

The Ego

The belief in separation — the original "sin," or error — is the origin and entire foundation of the *ego* — the illusion of a separated self, housed within a body, separate from other bodies and from God. The ego, the Course teaches, is nothing but a tiny fragment of our whole mind that has fallen asleep and is dreaming a terrifying nightmare in which it has sinned and thereby turned its Creator into a feared and hated enemy.

> *"This fragment of your mind is such a tiny part of it that, could you but appreciate the whole, you would see instantly that it is like the smallest sunbeam to the sun, or like the faintest ripple on the surface of the ocean. In its amazing arrogance, this tiny sunbeam has decided it is the sun; this almost imperceptible ripple hails itself as the ocean. Think how alone and frightened is this little thought, this infinitesimal illusion, holding itself apart against the universe. The sun becomes the sunbeam's 'enemy' that would devour it, and the ocean terrifies the little ripple and wants to swallow it.*
>
> *"Yet neither sun nor ocean is even aware of all this strange and meaningless activity. They merely continue, unaware that they are feared and hated by a tiny segment of themselves. Even that segment is not lost to them, for it could not survive apart from them. And what it thinks it is in no way changes its total dependence on them for its being. Its whole existence still remains in them. Without the sun the sunbeam would be gone; the ripple without the ocean is inconceivable...*
>
> *"Like to the sun and ocean your Self continues, unmindful that this tiny part regards itself as you.... This little aspect is no different from the whole, being continuous with it and at one with it. It leads no separate life, because its life is the oneness in which its being was created.*
>
> *"Do not accept this little, fenced-off aspect as yourself."*
> — T. pp. 364–65; T-18.VIII.3:3–6, 4,
> 6:1, 5, and 7:1

This passage is extremely important in understanding both the theory and the practice of the Course. The ego is not enemy to God and our own Self, to be hated, fought against, or destroyed. It is simply a tiny fragment of our own mind that has become deeply confused about what it is and terrified in that confusion. It has no power but the power of our own thought and belief. The ego is an illusion about our own nature and our relationship to our Source — an illusion that needs only to be returned to the light of truth, a mistaken belief that needs only to be gently corrected.

The ego's dream of separation is not real. And yet we have gone deeply into the dream and identified strongly with this illusion of ourselves. Just as our nighttime dreams seem very real to us while we are dreaming, the dream of separation feels very real to us. It is where we believe we are, and we perceive ourselves as the "hero," or central figure, of our dream. We have forgotten that we are the dreamer.

Our need is to awaken from the dream of separation and be restored to the awareness of Reality and our true Self. The journey home — our journey of healing — is a journey toward reawakening.

First Dream of Peace

"You will first dream of peace, and then awaken to it. Your first exchange of what you made for what you want is the exchange of nightmares for the happy dreams of love."
                                                    — T. p. 238; T-13.VII.9:1–2

We have all experienced what it is like to wake up suddenly from a nightmare. We bring the terror of the dream with us into the first moments of our being awake.

The Course teaches that this is not what God wills us. We have deeply invested in and identified with the ego's dream, and the dream is a terrifying one. God wills us a gentler awakening.

"You are the dreamer of the world of dreams. No other cause it has, nor ever will. Nothing more than an idle dream has terrified God's Son, and made him think that he has lost his innocence, denied his Father, and made war upon himself. So fearful is the dream, so seeming real, he could not waken to reality without the sweat of terror and

a scream of mortal fear, unless a gentler dream preceded his awaking, and allowed his calmer mind to welcome, not fear, the Voice That calls with love to waken him; a gentler dream, in which his suffering was healed and where his brother was his friend. God willed he waken gently and with joy, and gave him means to waken without fear.

— T. p. 542; T-27.VII.13

God's Love meets us where we are in our subjective experience — within the dream — and guides us gently toward the readiness to awaken by helping us transform our nightmare into a peaceful dream. We exchange our nightmare of sin, guilt, conflict, and fear for a dream of forgiveness, healing, and love.

When our dream comes to so closely reflect the peace, joy, and beauty of Heaven that the difference between sleep and waking is nearly imperceptible, the Course teaches that God Himself will take the final step to awaken us.

The means given us to transform our fearful dream — the means that is the central teaching and practice of the Course — is *forgiveness*. We learn forgiveness through the Teacher of forgiveness within our mind — the Holy Spirit.

The Holy Spirit

The Course teaches that the Holy Spirit is God's Answer to the ego, to the idea of separation. In the same instant that the separation *seemed* to occur, God placed the Holy Spirit within our minds. The Holy Spirit is the Voice for God. He is the memory of God's Love we carry deep within our minds and hearts, even within the dream. His presence in our minds belies the separation and undoes our mistaken belief that it is real.

He is our Guide to right seeing and right understanding, Who speaks only for the truth of what we are and what our brother is. He is Transformer of our misperceptions, Translator of our guilty, fearful dreams into happy dreams of forgiveness and peace.

The Parable of the Prodigal Son

"Ask not to be forgiven, for this has already been accomplished. Ask, rather, to learn how to forgive, and to restore what always was to your unforgiving mind."
— T. p. 260; T-14.IV.3:4–5

The parable of the prodigal son offers a full and rich metaphor for our journey of healing within the dream of separation.

"Listen to the story of the prodigal son, and learn what God's treasure is and yours: The son of a loving father left his home and thought he had squandered everything for nothing of any value, although he had not understood its worthlessness at the time. He was ashamed to return to his father, because he thought he had hurt him. Yet when he came home the father welcomed him with joy, because the son himself **was** *his father's treasure. He wanted nothing else."*
— T. p. 138; T-8.VI.4

Through this parable, Jesus teaches us clearly that there is no condemnation in God. The prodigal left home and wandered deep into the far country of illusion and despair. One morning, the story says, he awoke and "came to himself." He remembered that he had a home and a kind and loving father. He decided to go home.

The prodigal set out on his journey home believing that he had sinned against his father and that he was no longer worthy to be called his father's son. Yet when his father heard that he was coming, he sent an escort to meet him and make the journey of return with him. When the prodigal came before him, the father greeted him with unreserved welcome, joy, feasting, and celebration. In effect, the father said to his son, "You are mistaken in how you see yourself. You are still my son, my heart's treasure, whom I love and in whom I delight."

Only then did the prodigal come to understand that nothing had changed, nothing had been lost, nothing had destroyed his identity or his father's love.

The teaching of the parable does not end, however, with the prodigal's return. There was a second son, who had appeared to be "good" and to do everything his father wanted. This son became jealous and angry over his father's celebration of his brother's return and complained bitterly that his father had never held such a feast for him. He would have denied his brother welcome, pointing out his brother's "sins" and contrasting them with his own "righteousness."

Just as the father did not condemn the prodigal for his wanderings, neither did he become angry with his second son's bitterness and jealousy. He simply reminded this son, gently and lovingly, that all his, the father's, wealth was *also* his — *and always had been*. It was freely his for the accepting, just as it was being freely given his brother.

This son's belief that his father's favor and grace had to be *earned* shows that he did not really *know* his father's loving nature. That lack of understanding and his self-righteous stance had separated *him* from his father just as much as the prodigal's misguided wanderings had done. He too had denied himself the experience of his father's limitless abundance and love.

Regardless of the past, the second son's unforgiveness of his brother was all that kept him from fully sharing in the feast *now*. The unforgiveness in *our* minds is all that is keeping *us* from awakening and sharing in the overflowing richness of Creation.

It is not God's forgiveness that we need, for as this story makes clear, our Father has not condemned us. It is our own forgiveness that is needed, for we have banished ourselves from the awareness and experience of His Love. We receive the gifts of forgiveness as we are willing to extend forgiveness to our brother.

The challenge of our healing journey is twofold — for we are like *both* the prodigal son and the self-righteous son in this parable. Like the prodigal, we need to recognize that we cannot find fulfillment, happiness, safety, or peace in the ego's world, in all the misdirected ways and places we've sought for them. We can find our treasure only by remembering who we are, by coming home.

This is our deepest longing, our true heart's desire. Even in the midst of lostness and pain, for a moment we can "come to ourselves." We can glimpse a memory, however vague, of a home we dearly loved. We can hear it call softly to us in the longing of our heart, and we can decide to go home. In the holy instant of that decision, our journey has begun.

Then, like the second son, we must learn that whenever we would deny a brother his rightful place as God's Son, we also deny our own.

Only by our willingness to recognize and celebrate Who he is in truth — no matter how far he may seem to have strayed, no matter what he seems to have done — can we know our own Identity as well. We can share in the blessing that is ours only as one.

In this way our dream is transformed. In this way we are made ready for awakening.

"Dream softly of your sinless brother, who unites with you in holy innocence. And from this dream the Lord of Heaven will Himself awaken His beloved Son."

— T. p. 543; T-27.VII.15:1–2

Chapter 2

"You Are As God Created You"

"Salvation requires the acceptance of but one thought; — you are as God created you, not what you made of yourself."
— W. p. 160; W-Pt.I.93.7:1

One Saturday morning in January, my morning meditation was Workbook Lesson 224 from the Course.

"God is my Father, and He loves His Son."

"My true Identity is so secure, so lofty, sinless, glorious and great, wholly beneficent and free from guilt, that Heaven looks to It to give it light. It lights the world as well. It is the gift my Father gave to me; the one as well I give the world. There is no gift but This that can be either given or received. This is reality, and only This. This is illusion's end. It is the truth.

"My Name, O Father, still is known to You. I have forgotten it, and do not know where I am going, who I am, or what it is I do. Remind me, Father, now, for I am weary of the world I see. Reveal what You would have me see instead."
— W. p. 393; W-Pt.II.224

I was deeply moved by both the message and the prayer of this lesson. I had been going through a very difficult personal time, struggling within myself to face the truth that the love relationship in my life — a five-year marriage of the heart — was not working, not nourishing either of us in some very fundamental ways. Within a week I would somehow find the strength inside to confront the truth openly, make the choice to let go of the relationship, and enter a deeper process of relinquishment, transformation, and healing. But at that moment I felt paralyzed by conflict and fear.

I knew that I was very disconnected from any sense of the lofty Identity described in the lesson. I had forgotten my true Name. I felt very lost and confused about who I was, where I was going, and what I was doing. And I was crying out in weariness and pain to be reminded, to be shown the way to healing and to peace.

That same day I attended a workshop with Insight meditation teacher Jack Kornfield, author of *A Path with Heart: A Guide through the Perils and Promises of Spiritual Life*. During the workshop, Dr. Kornfield shared a story that stirred something — a memory, a longing — deep in my heart.

There is a village somewhere in Africa, he told us, that counts the birthday of a child, not from the day the child is born into physical existence, not even from the day the child is conceived in the womb, but from the day the child is born *as a thought in his mother's mind.*

One day a woman in the village has the thought, "I will have a child with my mate." She then goes apart from the village and sits under a tree. She sits, listening, until inside herself she hears the song that is the song of this child who would come into being through her. Once she has heard the song, she sings it to herself again and again until she knows it. Then she returns to her home and teaches the song to her mate. They sing it together while making love, inviting the child to be born of their union.

Later the song is taught to the midwives, who sing it to the child during and immediately after the birth process, to welcome him to life. And the song is taught to all the people of the village. Then if the child is playing and falls down, whoever is nearby can pick him up and comfort him by singing his song to him. This song is sung throughout his life, at all rites of passage, and is sung finally as his earthly life comes to its end.

When Dr. Kornfield finished telling this story, there was a profound silence and stillness in the room. Everyone felt touched by a nameless sense of recollection and longing and by the recognition that we all shared this same response.

What touches the heart so deeply about this story, I believe, is that we all know, on some level, that we too have a song — a song of our creation, a song we long to sing and to hear sung. How wonderful it must be, Dr. Kornfield reflected, to be part of a community in which everyone knows your song and sings it to you, in affirmation and celebration of your truth and your being.

An ancient song in our hearts, nearly forgotten, calls us to remembrance of the deepest truth in us, to the Self who is born and reborn and lives eternally as a Thought in the Mind of God.

Our True Self — The Thought God Holds of Us

"The Thought of God created you. It left you not, nor have you ever been apart from it an instant. It belongs to you. By it you live. It is your Source of life, holding you one with it, and everything is one with you because it left you not. The Thought of God protects you, cares for you, makes soft your resting place and smooths your way, lighting your mind with happiness and love. Eternity and everlasting life shine in your mind, because the Thought of God has left you not, and still abides with you."

— W. p. 306; W-Pt.I.165.2

While we wander here, lost in our dream of separation and exile, our song is a song of deep yearning, of profound longing for our home — a home we have nearly forgotten, yet which calls us, unceasingly, to return. The Sufis call this longing the "Divine *Ishq*" — the "divine nostalgia," or homesickness for our true nature and source.

The Course speaks to us of a love song being sung between Creator and Creation, Father and Son, in every instant. In its fullness and celebration, its communion and joy, is Heaven itself. When we are very quiet, very still inside, we can hear something of that ancient song.

"Listen, — perhaps you catch a hint of an ancient state not quite forgotten; dim, perhaps, and yet not altogether unfamiliar, like a song whose name is long forgotten, and the circumstances in which you heard completely unremembered. Not the whole song has stayed with you, but just a little wisp of melody, attached not to a person or a place or anything particular. But you remember, from just this little part,

*how lovely was the song, how wonderful the setting where you heard
it, and how you loved those who were there and listened with you.*

*"The notes are nothing. Yet you have kept them with you, not
for themselves, but as a soft reminder of what would make you weep
if you remembered how dear it was to you. You could remember, yet
you are afraid, believing you would lose the world you learned since
then. And yet you know that nothing in the world you learned is half
so dear as this. Listen, and see if you remember an ancient song you
knew so long ago and held more dear than any melody you taught
yourself to cherish since."*

— T. pp. 416–17; T-21.I.6, 7

The spiritual journey, regardless of the particular path we follow,
is a journey of *remembrance* — a reawakening to the Self, which is
eternal, changeless, radiant. The journey to our Self *is* the journey
to God.

*"Can you be separated from your life and your being? The journey
to God is merely the reawakening of the knowledge of where you are
always, and what you are forever. It is a journey without distance to
a goal that has never changed."*

— T. p. 139; T-8.VI.9:5–7

Our true Self is not changed by our forgetting or our dreams. We
remain forever as we were created — a pure and perfect Thought in
the Mind of our Father.

*"The Thought God holds of you is perfectly unchanged by your for-
getting. It will always be exactly as it was before the time when you
forgot, and will be just the same when you remember. And it is the
same within the interval when you forgot."*

— T. p. 587; T-30.III.7:6–8

With our limited human comprehension, we cannot begin to truly
grasp the vastness, brilliance, and beauty of the Thought God holds of
us. But sometimes words, images, visions — like the dimly heard notes
of a nearly forgotten song — point us in the direction of remembrance.

As you read this description from the Course, see if you do not feel some kind of inner response, some stirring of an ancient recognition deep, deep within you.

> *"The Thoughts of God are far beyond all change, and shine forever. They await not birth. They wait for welcome and remembering. The Thought God holds of you is like a star, unchangeable in an eternal sky. So high in Heaven is it set that those outside of Heaven know not it is there. Yet still and white and lovely will it shine through all eternity. There was no time it was not there; no instant when its light grew dimmer or less perfect ever was.*
>
> *"... Completely unaffected by the turmoil and the terror of the world, the dreams of birth and death that here are dreamed, the myriad of forms that fear can take; quite undisturbed, the Thought God holds of you remains exactly as it always was. Surrounded by a stillness so complete no sound of battle comes remotely near, it rests in certainty and perfect peace. . . . In perfect sureness of its changelessness and of its rest in its eternal home, the Thought God holds of you has never left the Mind of its Creator, Whom it knows as its Creator knows that it is there."*
>
> — T. pp. 587–88; T-30.III.8, 10:2–3, 5

There *is* a place within us of calm, of perfect peace — a place beyond the dramas of our lives, beyond the grasping and cherishing of the self we think we are. We may touch that place only briefly, only occasionally, but we have all had at least a moment of sensing that there is something greater, something deeper, something beyond all the concerns and preoccupations that usually loom so large in our focus, something more real and lasting than the fleeting pleasures, pains, experiences, and life of the body. We have all touched or glimpsed or felt something of the Self, and we can never completely forget. It calls us to return.

The Ego's Evaluation of What We Are

The memory of our true Identity remains in our minds and is reflected in the Holy Spirit's perception and evaluation of who and what we are. Within the dream of separation, however, there seems to be another evaluation in our minds as well — the ego's perception and teaching of what we are.

> *"It is perfectly obvious that if the Holy Spirit looks with love on all He perceives, He looks with love on you. His evaluation of you is based on His knowledge of what you are, and so He evaluates you truly. And this evaluation must be in your mind, because He is. The ego is also in your mind, because you have accepted it there. Its evaluation of you, however, is the exact opposite of the Holy Spirit's, because the ego does not love you. It is unaware of what you are, and wholly mistrustful of everything it perceives because its perceptions are so shifting. The ego is therefore capable of suspiciousness at best and viciousness at worst. That is its range. It cannot exceed it . . . "*
>
> — T. pp. 163–64; T-9.VII.3:1–9

We do not experience and identify with our reality — the Thought God holds of us, the Self — because we have accepted instead the self born of the ego, born of the thought of separation and sin. Sin is defined by the Course as *"lack of love"* (T. p. 9; T-1.IV.3:1), and the ego's picture of what we are is profoundly unloving.

> *"You think you are the home of evil, darkness and sin. You think if anyone could see the truth about you he would be repelled, recoiling from you as if from a poisonous snake. You think if what is true about you were revealed to you, you would be struck by horror so intense that you would rush to death by your own hand, living on after seeing this being impossible."*
>
> — W. p. 161; W-Pt.I.93.1

This picture of ourselves, with all its ugliness, guilt, and horror, lies at the very core of the ego thought system. It is what we all, deep down, believe to be true about us, and what the ego has convinced us we dare not look at directly. Projection arises from our need to try to escape this picture of ourselves by seeing it outside of us, in someone or something else. We then put on what the Course calls the *"face of innocence"* as a compensation, a mask to further distance ourselves from what we believe to be the terrible truth of what we are.

The "Face of Innocence"

The face of innocence is a part of the self-concept everyone caught up in this world of separation, in the split mind, makes and defends. The Course describes the dynamics of the face of innocence this way:

"A concept of the self is made by you. It bears no likeness to yourself at all. It is an idol, made to take the place of your reality as Son of God. The concept of the self the world would teach is not the thing that it appears to be. For it is made to serve two purposes, but one of which the mind can recognize. The first presents the face of innocence, the aspect acted on. It is this face that smiles and charms and even seems to love. It searches for companions and it looks, at times with pity, on the suffering, and sometimes offers solace. It believes that it is good within an evil world.

"This aspect can grow angry, for the world is wicked and unable to provide the love and shelter innocence deserves. And so this face is often wet with tears at the injustices the world accords to those who would be generous and good. This aspect never makes the first attack. But every day a hundred little things make small assaults upon its innocence, provoking it to irritation, and at last to open insult and abuse.

"The face of innocence the concept of the self so proudly wears can tolerate attack in self-defense, for is it not a well-known fact the world deals harshly with defenseless innocence? No one who makes a picture of himself omits this face, for he has need of it. The other side he does not want to see."

— T. p. 610; T-31.V.2, 3, 4:1–3

The face of innocence is our investment in seeing ourselves as innocent and helpless victims of the world we see around us. Our own anger and attacks on the world — even to the point of rage and viciousness — are portrayed as "justified," as originating outside of ourselves, provoked and caused by someone other than and different from ourselves. We are not responsible for the ugliness in ourselves; our brother is.

"Beneath the face of innocence there is a lesson that the concept of the self was made to teach. It is a lesson in terrible displacement, and

a fear so devastating that the face that smiles above it must forever look away, lest it perceive the treachery it hides. The lesson teaches this: 'I am the thing you made of me, and as you look on me, you stand condemned because of what I am.' On this conception of the self the world smiles with approval, for it guarantees the pathways of the world are safely kept, and those who walk on them will not escape.

"Here is the central lesson that ensures your brother is condemned eternally. For what you are has now become his sin. For this no forgiveness is possible. No longer does it matter what he does, for your accusing finger points to him, unwavering and deadly in its aim. It points to you as well, but this is kept still deeper in the mists below the face of innocence. And in these shrouded vaults are all his sins and yours preserved and kept in darkness, where they cannot be perceived as errors, which the light would surely show."

— T. pp. 610–11; T-31.V.5, 6:1–6

An Example

I once saw a television documentary about a rehabilitation program being offered for prisoners who had committed violent crimes. This program was entirely voluntary and carried no "points" toward either parole or other privileges. As a result, those men participating in the program were there because of a genuine desire for some kind of healing and change.

The program involved bringing family members of people who had been victims of violent crime (though not at the hands of these particular prisoners) into a room with the prisoners — either live or through videotape — and having them share the impact on their lives of that experience. The sharing was neither blaming nor accusatory, but simply a sharing from the heart of the human pain and suffering they and their families had experienced. At first the prisoners would defend against what they were hearing in various ways — acting tough, making wisecracks, feigning disinterest. But little by little they softened and began to experience the deep pain and guilt they were living with within themselves. Many broke down and wept.

One prisoner who was interviewed shared that he had never before thought of the man he had attacked and robbed as a human being, with feelings and a family who loved and cared about him. He had never thought of that man as a victim — because, he explained, he had been completely caught up in seeing *himself* as the victim, of an unjust and uncaring society. And so, in his mind, what he was doing was fully justified and wholly unquestioned. Society was responsible for what he did and what he had become, not himself. Yet underneath, the tremendous guilt he had denied and projected — that he had now begun to get in touch with — was devastating.

This is a very striking illustration of how powerful a hold this dynamic — presenting the face of innocence and projecting the source of our guilt — has on our psyche. It is also a clear illustration of the fact that these ego defenses preserve and reinforce the very guilt they seem to protect us from.

This particular prisoner had taken the first step toward healing by recognizing and withdrawing his projection of guilt onto society. The Course cautions that this process is apt to be painful, because we are still convinced that our guilt is real.

> *"The beginning phases of this reversal are often quite painful, for as blame is withdrawn from without, there is a strong tendency to harbor it within. It is difficult at first to realize that this is exactly the same thing, for there is no distinction between within and without.*
>
> *"... blame must be undone, not seen elsewhere. Lay it to yourself and you cannot know yourself, for only the ego blames at all. Self-blame is therefore ego identification, and as much an ego defense as blaming others. You cannot enter God's Presence if you attack His Son."*
>
> — T. p. 187; T-11.IV.4:5–6, 5:3–6

Only as we are willing to reclaim our projections of guilt and look clearly and open-eyed at the picture the ego paints of us can the Holy Spirit within us teach us that this picture is not true. That is His function in our minds. As we are willing to bring all the darkness of the ego to the Holy Spirit, to be looked at with Him in the light of truth, the darkness is dispelled and the glory of our true Self revealed to us.

Chapter 3

Accepting Our True Identity

"The self you made is not the Son of God. Therefore, this self does not exist at all. And anything it seems to do and think means nothing. It is neither bad nor good. It is unreal, and nothing more than that."
— W. p. 159; W-Pt.I.93.5:1–5

"Where could the Thought God holds of you exist but where you are? Is your reality a thing apart from you, and in a world which your reality knows nothing of?... You have not two realities, but one. Nor can you be aware of more than one. An idol or the Thought God holds of you is your reality. Forget not, then, that idols must keep hidden what you are, not from the Mind of God, but from your own. The star still shines; the sky has never changed. But you, the holy Son of God Himself, are unaware of your reality."
— T. p. 588; T-30.III.11:1–2, 5–10

Our journey here is a journey to the remembrance of our true Identity, a journey of reawakening to Who we really are. Henri J. M. Nouwen, in *Life of the Beloved*, describes this as a process of daring to accept, express, and fully live our identity as the Beloved, the holy Son of God.

"... being the Beloved is the origin and the fulfillment of the life of the Spirit. I say this because, as soon as we catch a glimpse of this truth, we are put on a journey in search of the fullness of that truth and we will not rest until we can rest in that truth. From the moment we claim the truth of being the Beloved, we are faced with the call

41

*to become who we are. Becoming the Beloved is the great spiritual
journey we have to make."*

— Henri J. M. Nouwen,
Life of the Beloved, p. 37

The memory of our real Self, our true Identity, remains within our
mind and calls to us in the deepest recesses of our mind and heart. We
cannot help but undertake the journey, the search for the wholeness
and innocence we believe we have lost.

*"I can only look for something that I have, to some degree, already
found. How can I search for beauty and truth unless that beauty and
truth are already known to me in the depths of my heart?... We were
innocent before we started feeling guilty; we were in the light before
we entered into the darkness; we were at home before we started to
search for a home. Deep in the recesses of our minds and hearts there
lies a treasure we seek. We know its preciousness, and we know that
it holds the gift we most desire...."*

— Henri J. M. Nouwen,
Life of the Beloved, p. 38

*"You will undertake a journey here because you are not at home in this
world. And you will search for your home whether you realize where
it is or not. If you believe it is outside you the search will be futile, for
you will be seeking it where it is not. You do not remember how to look
within for you do not believe your home is there. Yet the Holy Spirit
remembers it for you, and He will guide you to your home because that
is His mission. As He fulfills His mission He will teach you yours, for
your mission is the same as His. By guiding your brothers home you
are following Him."*

— T. pp. 208–9; T-12.IV.5:1–5

We can come home to ourselves, we can reclaim our true Identity, only by being willing to undertake a journey of *looking within.* We
fear this process because we have accepted into our minds not only the
truth of Who we are as God created us, but a false image of ourselves
as well. Our minds are split and contain two evaluations of who and
what we are.

The Two Evaluations

In the last chapter we began to explore the two evaluations of who and what we are that are contained within our split mind. The loftiness of the Holy Spirit's perception of us, which glimpses our reality as God created us, is literally beyond our imagining. The Course hints at it, however, in a number of Workbook lessons. For instance,

"The Son of God is my Identity"

"My Self is holy beyond all the thoughts of holiness of which I now conceive. Its shimmering and perfect purity is far more brilliant than is any light that I have ever looked upon. Its love is limitless, with an intensity that holds all things within it, in the calm of quiet certainty. Its strength comes not from burning impulses which move the world, but from the boundless Love of God Himself. How far beyond this world my Self must be, and yet how near to me and close to God!"
— W. p. 410; W-Pt.II.252.1

By contrast, we saw that the picture the ego paints of us is a picture of sin, guilt, hatred, fear, and death — a picture so terrifying that we defend against it by projecting onto others. We are willing to recognize our own anger and viciousness only insofar as we can blame someone else for it, only as long as we can maintain our own *"face of innocence."* (T. pp. 610f; T-31.V) And yet, we saw, we purchase this illusion of innocence at the cost of reinforcing the seeming reality of our guilt and burying it deeper, rendering it even less accessible to dissolution and healing.

What allows these two evaluations of ourselves to both remain within our minds is the process of *dissociation*, of keeping them split off and apart from each other. The Course describes the nature of dissociation this way:

"Dissociation is a distorted process of thinking whereby two systems of belief which cannot coexist are both maintained. If they are brought together, their joint acceptance becomes impossible. But if one is kept in darkness from the other, their separation seems to keep them both alive and equal in their reality. Their joining thus becomes the source of fear, for if they meet, acceptance must be withdrawn from one of them.

You cannot have them both, for each denies the other. Apart, this fact is lost from sight, for each in a separate place can be endowed with firm belief. Bring them together, and the fact of their incompatibility is instantly apparent. One will go, because the other is seen in the same place."

— T p. 267; T-14.VII.4:3–10

The process of unmasking the ego and looking clearly at what we have identified with as our self can initially be horrifying. For, as Ken Wapnick has repeatedly pointed out in his teaching, "the ego is not a very pretty picture." And as the Course points out, we *are not guiltless in time, but in eternity"* (T. p. 221; T-13.I.3:2).

We have all thought, said, and done things in this world that are deeply unloving to others and to ourselves. We have all gotten caught up in vicious circles of attack and defense, judgment and punishment. We have all engaged in *"the treachery of specialness"* (T. p. 466; T-24.I), seeking for and bowing before idols we've made to take the place of God. And it is exactly these things that we are asked to look at, this inner darkness we are asked to bring to the light.

"That you have made mistakes is obvious. That you have sought salvation in strange ways; have been deceived, deceiving, and afraid of foolish fantasies and savage dreams; and have bowed down to idols made of dust, — all this is true by what you now believe.

"Today we question this, not from the point of view of what you think, but from a very different reference point, from which such idle thoughts are meaningless. These thoughts are not according to God's Will. These weird beliefs [that you hold about yourself] He does not share with you. This is enough to prove that they are wrong, but you do not perceive that this is so. . . .

"Salvation requires the acceptance of but one thought; — you are as God created you, not what you made of yourself. Whatever evil you may think you did, you are as God created you. Whatever mistakes you made, the truth about you is unchanged. Creation is eternal and un-alterable. Your sinlessness is guaranteed by God. You are and forever will be exactly as you were created."

— W. pp. 159–60; W-Pt.I.93.2:2–3, 3, and 7:1–6

As long as we try to hide from the darkness, ugliness, and pain of the ego, either through denial or projection, we keep it split off from healing. Only as we are willing to look, with neither judgment nor defense, at what we secretly believe to be true about ourselves, can our illusions be dispelled, our mistakes be corrected and their consequences in our experience undone, and the truth of what we are be revealed to us.

And so the healing process of the Course — and the way in which we can come to reclaim our true Identity — is one of bringing illusions to the truth, of bringing darkness to the light.

Bringing Darkness to the Light

"The Holy Spirit asks of you but this; bring to Him every secret you have locked away from Him. Open every door to Him, and bid Him enter the darkness and lighten it away. At your request He enters gladly. He brings the light to darkness if you make the darkness open to Him. But what you hide He cannot look upon. He sees for you, and unless you look with Him He cannot see. The vision of Christ is not for Him alone, but for Him with you. Bring, therefore, all your dark and secret thoughts to Him, and look upon them with Him. He holds the light, and you the darkness. They cannot coexist when both of you together look on them. His judgment must prevail, and He will give it to you as you join your perception to His."

— T. p. 268; T-14.VII.6

The ego has convinced us that if we ever came before God with all the guilty, shameful, hateful thoughts and feelings we harbor within our minds, we would be condemned and destroyed. Yet the Course teaches that it is always we ourselves — the ego part of our own mind — who judge ourselves so unmercifully. The Holy Spirit would never do so — and in fact always reverses the ego's judgment against us.

"The ego speaks in judgment, and the Holy Spirit reverses its decision, much as a higher court has the power to reverse a lower court's decisions in this world.... Being afraid, you do not appeal to the Higher Court because you believe its judgment would also be against you...."

"You need not fear the Higher Court will condemn you. It will merely dismiss the case against you. There can be no case against a child of God, and every witness to guilt in God's creations is bearing false witness to God Himself. Appeal everything you believe gladly to God's Own Higher Court, because it speaks for Him and therefore speaks truly. It will dismiss the case against you, however carefully you have built it up. The case against you may be fool-proof, but it is not God-proof. The Holy Spirit will not hear it, because He can only witness truly. His verdict will always be 'thine is the Kingdom,' because He was given to you to remind you of what you are."

— T. pp. 80, 81; T-5.VI.4:1, 7, 10

The Course makes very clear, over and over again, that it is not *our* function but the Holy Spirit's to undo our perception and experience of guilt and replace it with the vision that sees only the face of Christ in ourselves and our brothers. It is our function to *want* that healing and to be willing to ask Him to *look with us* at what we believe to be true about our brothers and ourselves.

This process, of replacing the ego's harsh judgment with the healing perception of the Holy Spirit, is what the Course means by forgiveness.

Forgiveness and Remembering Who We Are

*"In our remembrance of each other
lies our remembrance of God."*

— T. p. 135; T-8.IV.7:6

Forgiveness is the process by which we are restored to the awareness of our true Identity. It is a process of bringing illusion to truth and darkness to light. Ken Wapnick has summarized the process of forgiveness as involving three essential steps (Kenneth Wapnick, *A Talk Given on A Course in Miracles*, 3rd edition, pp. 69–73).

We have already said that one of the primary ways we attempt to hide from the darkness of sin, guilt, and fear we believe is within us is through projection. In other words, we see the darkness outside of us instead of inside. The first step in forgiveness is to take back our projection of guilt — that is, to recognize that the guilt we see and condemn in someone else is what we really believe, on a deeper level, to be lurking within us. In other words, we admit that the problem, the darkness, is not outside of us but in our own mind.

This step can be very painful and frightening for us. After all, it was our fear of seeing this inside ourselves that led us to project it out in the first place. To now acknowledge that we are looking in a mirror as we look at this one we have condemned brings us face to face with that awful picture of ourselves that we despise and fear.

This brings us to the second step of the process, which is "to look at our own guilt and all our feelings of self-hatred" (Wapnick, *A Talk Given*, p. 71). The real source of our fear and pain is not what we see — either outside or within — but rather that we *interpret and judge* what we see as being evil and deserving of punishment or attack. The second step in forgiveness is to accept responsibility for this interpretation and judgment as a *choice* we are making. It is the choice to see myself (reflected through my brother) as a son of the ego rather than a Son of God. Because it is a choice I am making, I can also decide that I do not want to make that choice. I can choose instead that I want another possibility, another understanding, another way to see.

The first two steps, then, in bringing the darkness to the light are to say, first, that the problem is not *outside* of me but *inside* and, second, that the problem is not in *what I am looking at* but in *how I am looking at it*. As we begin to understand that it is our decision to see our brother and our self as guilty that is causing us pain, we become willing to ask for help to change our minds. The third step is set in motion by this willingness.

The third step belongs to the Holy Spirit, and the Course is quite clear that it is His function and not our own. Through Him a different perception, understanding, or experience is given us — or spontaneously occurs to us — that releases us from guilt and dissolves our fear. It is His function to undo our guilt. It is our function to recognize that we have accepted the belief in guilt into our minds, that we have chosen to accept the ego's version of what we are in place of the Self that God created. It is our function to decide that we no longer want to see ourselves that way. And it is our function to ask His help to correct that perception.

"... let the Voice for God alone be Judge of what is worthy of your own belief. He will not tell you that your brother should be judged by what your eyes behold in him, nor what his body's mouth says to your ears, nor what your fingers' touch report of him. He passes by such idle witnesses, which merely bear false witness to God's Son. He recognizes only what God loves, and in the holy light of what He sees do all the ego's dreams of what you are vanish before the splendor He beholds.

"... thus He judges you. Accept His Word for what you are, for He bears witness to your beautiful creation, and the Mind Whose Thought created your reality."

— W. p. 272; W-Pt.I.151.7, 9:1–2

It is His light that shines away the darkness of the ego. It is His light in which we see the truth about our brother and about ourselves. It is this that teaches us the self we made is meaningless and has done nothing to change the deeper reality of the Christ within us. In this we are healed.

The Course teaches that *"forgiveness is an earthly form of love"* (W. p. 344; W-Pt.I.186.14:2). Through forgiving our illusions about who and what we are, we finally remember the Love that is our true Identity, our shared Identity with each other and with our Father and Source.

"Love is what binds us together. And what is love? Love is the ability of the Christ in me to speak to the Christ in you. Love is the ability of the Christ in me to recognize and bear witness to the Christ in you. Love is the ability to know that God is just as much your life as He is my life. Love is the ability to recognize that God's grace is bestowed upon you as well as upon me. Every truth that I know about me is the truth I know about you, and that is how I love you — by knowing God's truth about you."

— Joel Goldsmith, *Gift of Love,*
pp. 46–47

To hold up a mirror for each other of our deepest innocence and holiness through forgiveness is the greatest gift of healing we can offer.

*"... all I want to say to you is, 'You are the Beloved,' and all I hope is
that you can hear these words as spoken to you with all the tenderness
and force that love can hold. My only desire is to make these words
reverberate in every corner of your being — 'You are the Beloved.'
The greatest gift my friendship can give to you is the gift of your
Belovedness. I can give the gift only insofar as I have claimed it for
myself. Isn't that what friendship is all about: giving each other the
gift of our Belovedness?"*

— Henri J. M. Nouwen,
Life of the Beloved, p. 26

"All Things Are Echoes of the Voice for God"

The Course teaches that there is a way to look at *everything*
that happens in our experience here that lets it be for us a step toward remembrance, healing, and accepting our true Identity. Every
relationship, every situation, every problem in our lives can either reinforce our ego identification or offer us release from the pain of our
illusions.

The Holy Spirit is our Guide to right seeing and right understanding. There is nothing He cannot use for our healing, if we are willing
to let Him be our teacher.

*"Let Him be Judge as well of everything that seems to happen to you
in this world. His lessons will enable you to bridge the gap between
illusions and the truth.*

*"He will remove all faith that you have placed in pain, disaster,
suffering and loss. He gives you vision which can look beyond these
grim appearances, and can behold the gentle face of Christ in all of
them. You will no longer doubt that only good can come to you who
are beloved of God, for He will judge all happenings, and teach the
single lesson that they all contain.*

*"He will select the elements in them which represent the truth,
and disregard those aspects which reflect but idle dreams. And He
will reinterpret all you see, and all occurrences, each circumstance, and
every happening that seems to touch on you in any way from His*

frame of reference, wholly unified and sure. And you will see the love beyond the hate, the constancy in change, the pure in sin, and only Heaven's blessing on the world."

— W. p. 272; W-Pt.I.151.9:6–7, 10, 11

The Holy Spirit offers us a perception, an understanding, that sees through and past our false self-concepts and helps us hear once again the "forgotten song" of our true Self.

"Such is your resurrection, for your life is not a part of anything you see. It stands beyond the body and the world, past every witness for unholiness, within the Holy, holy as Itself. In everyone and every-thing His Voice would speak to you of nothing but your Self and your Creator, Who is one with Him. So will you see the holy face of Christ in everything, and hear in everything no sound except the echo of God's Voice."

— W. pp. 272–73; W-Pt.I.151.12

Accepting Our True Identity

"You are the work of God, and His work is wholly lovable and wholly loving. This is how a man must think of himself in his heart, because this is what he is."

— T. p. 7; T-1.III.2:3

"Father, I made an image of myself, and it is this I call the Son of God. Yet is creation as it always was, for Your creation is unchangeable. Let me not worship idols. I am he my Father loves. My holiness remains the light of Heaven and the Love of God. Is not what is beloved of You secure? Is not the light of Heaven infinite? Is not Your Son my true Identity, when You created everything that is?"

— W. p. 429; W-Pt.II.283.1

Our true Identity — who we are as the Beloved, the Son of God — remains unchanged and unchangeable by anything our egos believe we have done or ever could do. Our entire journey of healing is but the relearning of this simple truth.

God asks nothing more of us than that we accept this, and be glad.

*"O God
help me
to believe
the truth about myself
no matter
how beautiful it is!"*

— Macrina Wiederkehr,
Seasons of Your Heart, p. 71

Chapter 4

Forgiveness Is a Choice

Choosing What We See

"Forgiveness is a choice. I never see my brother as he is, for that is beyond perception. What I see in him is merely what I wish to see because it stands for what I want to be the truth. It is to this alone that I respond, however much I seem to be impelled by outside happenings."
— W. p. 470; W-Pt.II.335.1:1–4

The heart of the teaching and practice of the Course is the process and experience of forgiveness. Forgiveness is the means by which the experience of separation is undone, the guilt and pain of the past are released, and fear is rendered causeless. It is the bridge to what the Course calls the "real world" — which is this world seen in a light so loving that it perfectly reflects Heaven.

The attainment of the real world is the necessary preparation for the final step of awakening from our dream of separation. The Course teaches that God will take this final step Himself once we are ready. We ready our minds to remember God — or more precisely, we let ourselves be restored to the awareness of our *eternal* readiness (T. p. 356; T-18.IV.5:11) — by allowing the Holy Spirit in our minds to guide us gently through the healing process of forgiveness.

Forgiveness bridges the gap between the ego self we believe we are and the Self that God created. As we are willing to offer forgiveness to others — to see past their illusions about themselves, to see past their fear and their defenses, to see past the mask of their ego to the spark of Divine Light that is the truth in them — we receive our own forgiveness as well.

This is a process and journey of healing everyone must undertake in one way or another, because in this world we all suffer the pain of forgetfulness. Like the prodigal son, we find ourselves in misery, deprivation, fear, and loss because we have forgotten that we are our Father's sons and daughters. And like the self-righteous son in the parable, our judgments against ourselves and others — judgments that declare God's children unworthy to re-enter their Father's house — merely block our own homecoming, our own acceptance of our Father's gifts to us. Yet our judgments and the self-righteous arrogance of our egos cannot keep us ultimately from being where God wills us to be. They can merely delay our *experience* of the richness of our Father's love.

Forgiveness reveals to us that we are still our Father's daughters and sons, no matter what the ego has taught us about ourselves. Each time we forgive, we are a step closer to home. And every step we take is upheld and strengthened by the power of God and by the efforts of all who take the journey with us.

> *"Sooner or later must everyone bridge the gap he imagines exists between his selves. Each one builds this bridge, which carries him across the gap as soon as he is willing to expend some little effort on behalf of bridging it. His little efforts are powerfully supplemented by the strength of Heaven, and by the united will of all who make Heaven what it is, being joined within it. And so the one who would cross over is literally transported there."*
>
> — T. p. 313; T-16.III.8:2–5

Forgiveness Is a Shift in Perspective

> *"The bridge itself is nothing more than a transition in the perspective of reality."*
>
> — T. p. 322; T-16.VI.7:1

Forgiveness, as the term is used in the Course, is an inner process, a change in *the way we are looking at* a situation and, as a result, a change in *what we see*. Gerald Jampolsky calls forgiveness "an inner correction that lightens the heart" (*Teach Only Love*, p. 110), a healing process by which we return to peace of mind by letting go of thoughts, interpretations, and judgments that are not helpful to us — that lead us deeper into feelings of separation, victimization, fearfulness, defensiveness, anger, guilt, powerlessness, and blame.

One helpful way to understand forgiveness is to think of what are called "figure-ground" drawings. These are line drawings in which two different images can be seen in the same drawing. Probably the best known of these is a drawing that can be seen either as two faces in profile looking at each other or as a wine goblet.

Generally, when we first look at a figure-ground drawing, we will see only one of the two images. Others may tell us the other image is there as well, may even try to point it out to us — but until we actually *see* it we cannot really grasp what they are talking about. We may *believe* them — and certainly the second image is already there in the picture — but until we see it for ourselves, it isn't real to us, it doesn't exist for us in our experience.

What is necessary in order to see the second image in a figure-ground drawing is to let go of our definition, our idea of what we are looking at. We need to let go of the mind-set that has interpreted what our eyes are physically seeing in a particular way. Letting go, we essentially return our perception to a state of innocence, of not knowing what we are looking at. In that freshness and openness, we suddenly see the second image, as if it had been revealed to our sight. Once we've seen it, it is hard to imagine ever having not been able to see it that way.

Once we can see both images in a figure-ground drawing, we can continue to see either one. *But we cannot see both at once.* At any given moment we can see one image or the other, because that is the nature of perception. We can shift our perception back and forth between the two, but at any instant we are choosing to see and experience only one. To see one literally denies the other to our sight.

The Course teaches us that we need to look upon this world much like a figure-ground drawing — as neutral, lacking inherent meaning but reflecting back to us the meaning we want to see in it, what we want to experience as real for us. In any situation, in any person, we can see two different pictures — the picture the ego sees or the picture

the Holy Spirit sees. We can see either one. We can even see both —
but not at the same time. We must choose.

Choosing What We Would See

*"Two ways of looking at the world are in your mind, and your
perception will reflect the guidance you have chosen."*
                                        — T. pp. 214–15; T-12.VII.5:6

The two possible "pictures" we can see in any situation are illus-
trated by the story told in John 9, the story of the healing of the man
who was born blind.

*"As Jesus was walking along, he saw a man who had been born blind.
His disciples asked him, 'Teacher, whose sin caused him to be born
blind? Was it his own or his parents' sin?'*

*"Jesus answered, 'His blindness has nothing to do with his sins or
his parents' sins. He is blind so that God's power might be seen at
work in him. . . . '*

*"After he said this, Jesus spat on the ground and made some mud
with the spittle; he rubbed the mud on the man's eyes and told him,
'Go and wash your face in the Pool of Siloam.' So the man went,
washed his face, and came back seeing."*
                                        — John 9:1–3, 6–7

The picture the ego sees in any situation is a picture of guilt, a
picture of sin, a picture of unworthiness and punishment and fear.
This is clearly what the disciples were seeing as they looked at the
man who had been born blind. Although they *seemed* to be asking
Jesus a sincere question, they were really asking what the Course calls
a *"pseudo-question"* (T. p. 533; T-27.IV).

The disciples were, in fact, *making a statement*, disguised in the
form of a question. They had already decided what was going on in
this situation. They were certain that the man's blindness was punishment for sin, a sure sign of guilt. The only question left was: *Who* is
the guilty one — the man himself or his parents? They never called
into question their basic premise and assumption — that *someone* was
guilty and being punished.

Jesus' answer to them was that they were *looking at the situation incorrectly.* This was not a punishment, he said. It had nothing to do with sin, with anyone being guilty. Rather, it was an opportunity for the presence and power and love of God to be made manifest. Jesus offered them a different perception of the same facts, the same outer situation. They *could* choose to see it that way instead.

The man who was blind had a choice to make as well. He could perceive his blindness as the disciples did, as punishment and proof of guilt. Or he could share the interpretation, the way of seeing, that Jesus was offering — that this situation or problem in his life was *a means to become more aware of God's living presence and love,* and nothing else. That he did as Jesus instructed him symbolizes his willingness and choice to share Jesus' understanding and definition instead of that of the disciples. And in that choice — the willingness to accept what the Course calls the Vision of Christ — he accepted the healing given him. His blindness was undone, and he received the gift of true sight.

Perception and Choice

"Perception is a choice and not a fact."
— T. p. 425; T-21.V.1:7

These two mutually exclusive interpretations and ways of seeing are the only choices offered us in any situation — no matter how different the outer form and expression of these pictures may appear to be. Either we will see a symbol of separation — of sin, guilt, punishment, and fear — or we will see an opportunity for healing — a chance to become more aware of God's presence, power, and love. The first of these, the ego's perspective, is a picture of judgment and condemnation. The second, the perception of the Holy Spirit, is a picture of forgiveness and release.

As with a figure-ground drawing, we can see either of these pictures, and we may even alternate between the two. But we cannot see both at once. Choosing one hides the other from our sight. The question really is — Which do we prefer? Which one do we *want* to see?

"You see what you expect, and you expect what you invite. Your perception is the result of your invitation, coming to you as you sent for it. Whose manifestations would you see? Of whose presence would you be convinced? For you will believe in what you manifest...."
— T. p. 214; T-12.VII.5:1–5

In fact, neither of the two pictures we can see in a figure-ground drawing is any more "real" than the other. The drawing is no more, or less, a wine goblet than it is two faces looking at each other. The only meaningful criterion we have for deciding which picture to focus on is, Which do I prefer to see?

In a similar light, the Course teaches that forgiveness — being part of the illusory world of separation and needed only within that world — is itself an illusion. But the picture it shows us *points beyond* itself, beyond illusion, reminding us of the truth we have forgotten (W. p. 369; W-Pt.I.198.2, 3).

Forgiveness can be understood as the choice to see the picture the Holy Spirit would show us in a given situation — the choice to see our brother and sister and ourselves with the Vision of Christ instead of through the eyes of the ego. This choice, the Course teaches, releases us from the web of illusions rather than binding us deeper to them (W. p. 73; W-Pt.I.46.1).

This choice is possible to make in every situation where we are tempted to judge, separate, condemn. It is this we are here to learn.

"This is the lesson God would have you learn: There is a way to look on everything that lets it be to you another step to Him...."
— W. p. 359; W-Pt.I.193;13:1

"Let all your brother's errors be to you nothing except a chance for you to see the workings of the Helper given you to see the world He made instead of yours.... This world has much to offer to your peace, and many chances to extend your own forgiveness. Such its purpose is, to those who want to see peace and forgiveness descend on them, and offer them the light."
— T. p. 488; T-25.III.7:2, 8–9

The Choice to Forgive

The idea of choice, of preference in perception, is extremely important to understanding the practice of forgiveness.

Think for a moment about a situation or person you have not forgiven, about which you are carrying a grievance. As you bring this person or situation to mind, pay attention to how you feel. If you are honest with yourself, you are probably feeling some degree of physical or emotional discomfort, even pain. You may feel tense, angry, anxious, powerless, fearful, upset. Your stomach may be in knots, your blood pressure may rise, your breath may feel constricted, your heart may pound. You may be aware of a holding on, a tightening and gripping of the mind, a hardening and armoring of the heart. These feelings are the price we pay for unforgiveness.

The situation you are thinking about can be thought of — like everything else in this world — as a figure-ground drawing. It can show you evidence of someone's guilt, or it can be looked at as an opportunity to become more aware of God's healing presence, power, and love.

Just as when we first look at a figure-ground drawing we generally see one picture or the other, in any situation in which we are carrying a grievance, we are *already* focusing on and seeing the picture of guilt — and experiencing the feelings that result from that perception. We need to ask ourselves these two simple questions: Is the picture I am looking at bringing me happiness, a sense of safety, peace of mind? *Do I like how I feel?*

The Course assures us that the picture that forgiveness would show us leads to a very different experience.

> *"What could you want forgiveness cannot give. Do you want peace? Forgiveness offers it. Do you want happiness, a quiet mind, a certainty of purpose, and a sense of worth and beauty that transcends the world? Do you want care and safety, and the warmth of sure protection always? Do you want a quietness that cannot be disturbed, a gentleness that can never be hurt, a deep, abiding comfort, and a rest so perfect it can never be upset?*
>
> *"All this forgiveness offers you, and more."*
> — W. p. 213; W-Pt.I.122.1, 2:1

Just as in a figure-ground drawing, the picture that would give us all of this can already be seen in the situation, exactly as it is. *Nothing outside of us has to change for us to have a new perception.* But in order to actually *see* the alternative, we have to be willing to let go of the way we have been looking at the situation, of our own ideas and interpretations, which in fact are causing us pain. The Course asks us simply,

> *"Do you prefer that you be right or happy?"*
> — T p. 573; T-29.VII.1:9

One picture brings us pain, the other offers peace. As it was for the disciples and the man born blind, the choice is ours to make. We are asked only to be honest about which choice we have made and whether we like the results it has brought us. If not, we can change our mind and choose again.

> *". . . whenever you have listened to His interpretation the results have brought you joy. Would you prefer the results of your interpretation, considering honestly what they have been? God wills you better."*
> — T. p. 310; T-16.II.7:5–7

Each time we choose the perception that forgiveness offers us, we take a step across the bridge that carries us from the world of illusion to the real world and the memory of home.

Chapter 5

The Bridge of Forgiveness

"Every brother you meet becomes a witness for Christ or for the ego, depending on what you perceive in him. Everyone convinces you of what you want to perceive. . . . Everything you perceive is a witness to the thought system you want to be true. Every brother has the power to release you if you choose to be free."

— T. pp. 191–92; T-11.V.18:1–4

Forgiveness is the bridge of healing that carries us from fear to love, pain to joy, loneliness and isolation to connectedness and communion, conflict and turmoil to peace. Forgiveness is the choice we make to look at a brother, or a situation, or ourselves, through eyes of love instead of through eyes of judgment — to share the perception of the Holy Spirit rather than that of the ego.

Identification with the ego has imprisoned us in a nightmare of separation, guilt, and fear. Yet our real Self, our true nature, calls us to awaken from our dream. Truth calls to us from the other side of the bridge — calls us to lay down our weapons of judgment and condemnation, our defenses of projection and denial, and instead to take our brother's hand and cross the bridge together to the Self we share. The way is clear. The way is forgiveness. And eventually we will all make that choice.

A Personal Meditative Experience

*"Your bridge is builded stronger than you think, and your foot is
planted firmly on it. Have no fear that the attraction of those who
stand on the other side and wait for you will not draw you safely
across. For you will come where you would be, and where your Self
awaits you."*

— T. p. 313; T-16.III.9

One morning, as I was meditating on Workbook Lesson 202 from
the Course, I had a very direct and powerful experience of this image
of forgiveness as a bridge. Lesson 202 reads:

*"I am not a body. I am free.
For I am still as God created me."*

1. (182) "I will be still an instant and go home."

*"Why would I choose to stay an instant more where I do not belong,
when God Himself has given me His Voice to call me home?"*

*"I am not a body. I am free.
For I am still as God created me."*

— W. p. 378; W-Pt.I.r.VI.202

As I reflected on the phrase *"where I do not belong,"* I understood
this to mean the states of mind that are not my true home. I do not
belong in fear. I do not belong in loneliness and pain. I do not belong
in anger and judgment and self-judgment. I do not belong in anxiety
and worry and despair. When I am experiencing these states of mind
and feeling, it is because *I have chosen* to be where I do not belong.
And all the while God is calling me to come home to Him, calling me
to peace, to certainty of love and care, and to joy.

But why would I choose instead to stay where I don't belong?

As if in answer to my question, I saw myself standing on the edge
of a cliff, on one side of a vast chasm. Jesus was standing on the other
side, wordlessly extending an invitation to join him there. A narrow
log was the only means of crossing I could see. But the thought of
stepping out onto the log filled me with a terror of falling into the
bottomless expanse below.

I then remembered having read about this same image in a magazine story some months before. The article was a survival story about a man and his dog who had been trapped in the mountains by a blizzard. They had come to just such a place on their journey to safety. The man had made it across the log to the other side. The dog, who was devoted to him, was in great conflict. He desperately wanted to follow his beloved master, but was too frightened to set out across the log. The story described him pacing frantically back and forth at the edge of the ravine, whimpering and crying, torn between his enormous fear and his deep love and longing. The man knew that he could not carry the dog across. He could do nothing but wait on the other side — wait in devotion and love — wait and call to the frightened creature, gently urging and encouraging him, soothing and assuring him.

I realized that at that moment on my own journey of healing, I was feeling very much like that dog. I was acutely aware of the deep and agonizing conflict I felt so often in my life between fear and love — of wanting so to follow in the way of the Master, yet feeling too frightened, time and again, to set out across the bridge, terrified of falling into the void, terrified that this would be my "death."

I remembered that, in the story, the dog did summon his courage to follow. When he reached the other side he was, the story said, wild with relief and celebration and joy! I thought, is that truly what awaits me too?

I somehow understood that what was before me now, symbolically, was the bridge of forgiveness, the bridge to the real world, and that the terror I was experiencing was what the Course describes as the "fear of redemption," the fear of love — of God's love for us and ours for him. For in the face of the reality of this love, the ego would cease to hold any attraction for us and we would simply lay it aside. Being so identified with the ego, we fear this with the fear of death.

"Under the ego's dark foundation is the memory of God, and it is of this that you are really afraid.... You realize that by removing the dark cloud [our thoughts of attack and guilt] that obscures it, your love for your Father would impel you to answer His call and leap into Heaven.... For still deeper than the ego's foundation, and much stronger than it will ever be, is your intense and burning love of God, and His for you. This is what you really want to hide....

"For you could not control your joyous response to the call of love if you heard it, and the whole world you thought you made would vanish.

"... You have built your whole insane belief system because you think you would be helpless in God's Presence, and you would save yourself from His Love because you think it would crush you into nothingness.... You think you have made a world which God would destroy; and by loving Him, which you do, you would throw this world away, which you **would.** *Therefore, you have used the world to cover your love, and the deeper you go into the blackness of the ego's foundation, the closer you come to the Love that is hidden there.* **And it is this that frightens you.**"

> — T. pp. 225–26; T-13.III.2:1, 6, 8; 3:3; 4:1, 3–5

The terror I felt was showing me that I *do* believe, on some level, that if I choose to follow in the way of Love, choose to fully join with the Love that Jesus represents, I risk being destroyed and disappearing into a vast nothingness. And yet my yearning to follow and join was also so great and the pain of being separated from Love so wrenching. In my meditation I broke down sobbing, crying out not to be left behind, stranded in my fear — calling out to Jesus for help to find the courage inside myself to reach for his hand and follow him.

I heard his calm and gentle encouragement and assurance that I was safe, that there was nothing to fear, that I simply needed to take the first step. I then saw that the core of my fear was that I did not trust myself to be able to make it across. I heard him say, "You may not trust yourself, but I have perfect trust in you." And suddenly I had a child in my arms, a child given into my care, who needed me to carry her across the bridge to safety. I felt a settling and a resolve taking shape inside, but I could also feel that it was colored with willfulness rather than being an expression of simple willingness and faith.

The image then changed, and there was a brother standing with me on the cliff. I saw that he longed deeply to cross the bridge, just as I did, and that he was very afraid, just as I was. My heart opened to him in compassion and love. I knew that if I took this brother's hand and offered him assurance and comfort and courage, I would find my own as well. I felt myself calm and certain, as I said to him, "Take my hand. We'll go across together."

I could not cross the bridge alone. But in my love for a brother — in my desire to help him and my recognition that his need was *exactly* the same as mine — I found that, in the very instant that I offered my hand to him, I could also reach Jesus' hand and let him lead us across the bridge together.

In that same instant, the bridge itself was transformed in my perception. What had been a rough and narrow log with no railings and no supports, over a terrifying abyss of dark and empty space, was now a smooth, comfortably wide stone bridge that stretched across a lily-pad pond to a lovely little island in the center. The bridge, the crossing, and the destination were no longer treacherous and fearful but rather were beautiful and serene.

I felt very moved by, and deeply grateful for, this experience in meditation, for the images and insights it offered me. I understood in a new and deeper way that I cannot return home, cannot cross the bridge to the real world, alone. I cannot remember God and Heaven without my brother. I cannot accept the love, support, and guidance God would offer me through the Holy Spirit except through the willingness to *share it* with my brother, who is like me in both his need and fear and his deep longing for safety and peace and home.

Recognizing That We Share the Ego

Unforgiveness always seeks to separate and make different. It focuses on and attacks the manifestations and mistakes of another's ego while protesting that *we* are not like that, *we* would never do such a thing, and so on. The first step in forgiveness often entails recognizing that we share the same insanity, the same basic ego thought system, as the person we are judging, even if we express it in a very different outer form.

Recently a friend and member of our Fellowship had a disquieting experience. As he left work one afternoon, a total stranger walked up to him on the street and punched him in the nose. Fortunately, he was not badly hurt and chose to view the incident as a wake-up call, looking to see what spiritual lesson he could learn from the experience. He was able to use the experience to deepen his own capacity for compassion.

This man's wife is a student of the Course and a member of a study group I facilitate in New York City. When she told us about this incident, we were all struck by how odd it seemed that someone would attack a complete stranger on the street, without provocation, for absolutely no reason. Certainly none of *us* would ever be likely to do *that*.

And yet, on closer look, we realized how often we do attack total strangers — in our minds. We get on a bus, look around, and mentally judge and attack how people look, how they are dressed. We overhear a conversation between strangers and inwardly criticize their opinions or the way they speak. We have an argument with our mate in the morning and then angrily lash out at the person who accidentally bumps against us getting off the subway. We are irritated and short-tempered with the harried postal clerk because the lines in the post office are so long. The list could go on and on. Somehow, we don't find *these* attacks on total strangers strange.

Certainly, in this world, there is a difference between physically punching someone and criticizing that person in our minds, and the outer consequences for each will differ. Forgiveness simply recognizes that the *same thought system* — the same insane idea that we can feel better by attacking someone else — gives rise to both actions. What we would judge and condemn in another is merely a more overt or extreme expression of the ego thinking we get caught in as well.

Unforgiveness looks at these manifestations of the ego's insanity, condemns them, and demands punishment. Forgiveness recognizes them as expressions of fear, as deeply pained calls for love. It hears the prodigal crying out to be reminded that he is still his Father's son. And it answers with love, with a perception that offers us the gentle certainty that our true identity can never change.

"The power of love is extraordinary, and it begins in the human heart and can travel to infinity. So I practice opening my heart, so that I can see the Divine in others. So that I can see beyond the package — which is all the stuff they're doing that's not to my liking — to the gift inside the package, the essence, the beauty buried under the fear — theirs or mine.

"For however unacceptable the package, there's always a Holy Miracle inside: inside the surly teenager sitting coldly across from me at dinner is a confused little boy yearning to become someone he's not, and too afraid to risk being who he is. Inside the angry mother yelling at her crying child in the supermarket is an overwhelmed woman, herself a crying child, bone-tired and bone-lonely.

"My heart, no stranger to suffering, can easily cross the bridge to another suffering heart, when I get my judgments out of the way."

> — Sheila Morgan, "The Divine Dance
> in Our Daily Life," in *Fellowship in
> Prayer,* October 1993

Forgiveness begins with a recognition that we share the same ego thought system — and thus the same need for correction, healing, and love — as the one we have been tempted to judge. But it cannot stop here or we will remain prodigals together, still separate from home and from our source.

"... true forgiveness is not the adopting of a morally superior position. Nor does it acknowledge someone else's cruelty and pronounce it acceptable, for to do this would be dishonest. Forgiveness sees that no real grounds for condemnation exist, and for that to happen, new grounds for innocence must be recognized. Certainly the person's behavior cannot be rationalized away. He did behave the way he behaved. Possibly another motivation can be attributed to his behavior, such as fear instead of selfishness, and although this can be a good first step, it is not sufficient in itself to allow us to see the splendor of God's light within him. Forgiveness is a gentle turning away from what we see with our body's eyes and a searching for the truth that lies beyond the individual's ego."

> — Gerald Jampolsky,
> *Teach Only Love,* p. 116

Chapter 6

Seeing beyond Our Masks
to Who We Really Are

*"Could you not look with greater charity
on whom God loves with perfect love?"*

— T. p. 310; T-16.II.7:8

*"Charity is a way of looking at another as if he had already gone
far beyond his actual accomplishments in time. Since his own thinking is faulty he cannot see the Atonement for himself, or he would
have not need of charity. The charity that is accorded him is both an
acknowledgment that he needs help, and a recognition that he will
accept it."*

— T. p. 23; T-2.V.10:1–3

Forgiveness begins with the recognition that we all share the
painful insanity of the ego's thought system and thus share the same
need for the gentle healing and correction of the Atonement. We
have forgotten who we are and in that forgetting believe that we have
changed our reality, our original nature as creations of God. Like the
prodigal son, we believe that we are no longer worthy to be called our
Father's daughters and sons.

Forgiveness is the means by which we learn that this painful belief
about ourselves is not true. As we forgive, we recognize that we too are
forgiven. As we are willing to see past the mistakes of others' egos —
willing to see their hearts of innocence, the light of Christ that shines
in them beyond their veils of forgetfulness and fear — we open to the

presence of that light in ourselves as well. And we begin to remember our Father, who loves us all with a perfect love.

> *"Forgiveness is the means by which we will remember. Through forgiveness the thinking of the world is reversed. . . . Holding no one prisoner to guilt, we become free. Acknowledging Christ in all our brothers, we recognize His presence in ourselves. Forgetting all our misperceptions, and with nothing from the past to hold us back, we can remember God."*
>
> — Preface, p. xiii

The world teaches that God's son is guilty, deserving of our condemnation and blame. In the mistakes and manifestations of our brother's ego it sees evidence for its judgment and does not raise its interpretation to question.

> *"An unforgiving thought is one which makes a judgment that it will not raise to doubt, although it is not true."*
>
> — W. p. 391; W-Pt.II.1.2:1

Unforgiveness always focuses on the *body* for its proof of guilt — pointing to something the body did, or failed to do, or, as in the case of the man born blind, to a condition of the body as proof and demonstration of guilt. And it demands some kind of retribution from the body — some punishment or change — as payment for release from guilt.

Forgiveness does not look to the body for proof of innocence, nor is it based on anything the body's eyes show us. Its vision does not stop with the body and its errors, but looks further and deeper to the light of God beyond.

To Forgive Is to Overlook

> *"To forgive is to overlook. Look, then, beyond error and do not let your perception rest upon it, for you will believe what your perception holds. Accept as true only what your brother is, if you would know yourself."*
>
> — T. p. 156; T-9.IV.1:2–4

It is easy to misunderstand this idea of overlooking error and to see it as encouraging psychological denial. Forgiveness does not ask us to deny the events and facts of this world, or to pretend that certain behaviors and actions have not occurred. To overlook means to *look beyond,* to look further and deeper than the behavior, than the outer layers and expressions of personality and defense that seem to separate us and make us different from one another.

Former Soviet leader Nikita Khrushchev was once giving a speech, when suddenly an angry voice in the audience demanded, "Where were you when Stalin was committing his atrocities?" The room fell into stunned silence. Khrushchev's gaze slowly scanned the audience. He asked, "Who said that? Stand up. Identify yourself." Fear gripped every heart. No one moved. No one answered. "My friend," said Khrushchev finally, "where you are right now [that is, too frightened to come forward] is just where I was when Stalin was in power."

To forgive is not to condone or approve of actions that are harmful and destructive within this world of form. Nor does the forgiveness process ask that we deny or ignore the level of our human experience. There is a saying,

"If a blind man steps on your toe, it still hurts."

At the ego level, the human level, that is certainly true. We need not pretend that the man didn't step on our toe or that it didn't hurt. To forgive does not mean we should let the man continue to stand on our toe because he is blind. Nor does it preclude taking action that will make it less likely to happen again.

Forgiveness merely sees that whatever our brother did that was unloving was an expression of *blindness.* When we are caught up in the insanity of the ego, we are, in a very real sense, blind. In our blindness we have all done things that were insensitive or unloving to others and to ourselves. As the Course points out, *"frightened people can be vicious"* (T. p. 33; T-3.I.4:2), and we have all at times acted hurtfully out of our fear.

Forgiveness does not close its eyes to such actions. But its vision does not stop at the outer appearances. Rather it sees past them to the terrible fear that underlies all attack, to the overwhelming guilt that hides behind all anger, to the profound pain and sense of worthlessness that give rise to all cruelty. It sees that behind all hurtful actions — no matter how extreme the form — stand, not monsters, but children of God lost in forgetfulness and fear — prodigal sons deeply mistaken about themselves and everyone around them, desperately calling out to be reminded of who they really are.

> "... *deep urges for goodness exist in everyone's heart no matter how overlayered they may be with guilt, defensiveness, dishonesty and in-humanity. Forgiveness looks past the more superficial motivations of the individual, no matter how extreme these may be, to the place in his heart where he yearns for exactly what we yearn for. Everyone wants peace and safety. Everyone wants to make a difference. And everyone wants to release his potential for love. It is deep into this desire that forgiveness gazes, and seeing there a reflection of itself, it releases the other from judgment.*"
>
> — Gerald Jampolsky,
> *Teach Only Love,* pp. 116–17

Just as we all share the insanity of the ego, so we all share the deep desire to go home — to be reunited with the Love that created us, the love that we are. Forgiveness hears our brother or sister afraid, crying out for love, and recognizes our own cry. And forgiveness answers our fear with love, recognizing that mistakes call for correction and learning, not condemnation and punishment.

> "*True forgiveness is based on reality.... The truth of our reality is that each of us is innocent and loved completely by God. It's not that we haven't made countless mistakes and will probably continue to do so for some time.... All mistakes come from the ego and are part of a learning process that everyone must go through. Forgiveness is a gentle vision that sees the maturity, the goodness of heart, and wholeness of character that will come in time to each person. And it recognizes the inappropriateness of condemnation to this growth process.*"
>
> — Gerald Jampolsky,
> *Teach Only Love,* pp. 111–12

No matter how different our paths may appear, we are all traveling the same journey of learning, healing, remembering. Forgiveness shows us a glimpse of what awaits us at journey's end, on the other side of the bridge, and gently urges us on.

Forgiveness Sees beyond the Masks We Wear to Who We Really Are

"I forgive, I forgive,
And I love you as you are.
I see the purity of your heart.
Behind the veils of who I think you are,
I see love, only love.
Behind the veils of who you think you are,
God sees love, only love."

— John Astin, "Forgiveness"
from *Into the Light*

Mother Teresa has often been asked how she is able to do the work she does with the destitute, the sick, the dying. Her answer expresses the very essence of true forgiveness. She says, "I see in each one the face of my beloved Lord, in all His distressing disguises."

Forgiveness is the vision that shows us the light of Christ shining behind the masks of separateness we wear. Our egos are very concerned with judging the masks — as pretty or ugly, acceptable or unacceptable, holy or sinful, attractive or grotesque. Forgiveness, the perception of the Holy Spirit, sees that they are all the same — they are all simply unreal. Behind each one stands the Christ, the One Self created by God, the true Identity we all share.

"To enrich our own life we must learn to give recognition to the true identity of those we meet. The person we meet today is presenting his Christhood for identification. He thinks he is presenting a sick body to be healed, a disturbed mind to be set at peace, an empty purse to be filled, or morals to be cleansed. But we know better.

"... we disregard the appearance of his humanhood and through spiritual discernment behold the Christ looking out of his eyes silently, sacredly, secretly.

"... whoever he is, he is presenting his Christhood for our acknowledgment. We may be faced with a gambler, a prostitute, a sick or dying person, but always he is presenting his Christhood to us for recognition and identification."

— Joel Goldsmith,
Gift of Love, pp. 15–16

To be identified with the ego is to have forgotten that we are wearing a mask, to confuse our masks with who we really are. We put enormous emphasis on getting our own and others' masks to look the way we think they should. In the sight of forgiveness, the appearance of the mask becomes irrelevant. For the mask itself becomes *transparent*, and the light of Christ shines through.

> *"Every time some person comes to us trying to convince us that he has a sick body, an empty purse, or is living a sinful life, we learn not to try to change the evil into good, not to pray that God take away the negative appearance and restore the positive. Rather, we ignore the appearance, look right through it, and see that behind the eyes of every individual is the Christ."*
>
> — Joel Goldsmith, *Gift of Love*, p. 16

Bridging the Distance — An Example

I recently read a beautiful description of this essence of true forgiveness in the book *How Can I Help?* by Ram Dass and Paul Gorman. It involved a woman whose father was dying of cancer. Because she lived a thousand miles away, her visits had been periodic. Near the end she was called to come suddenly. On entering his hospital room, she literally did not recognize the man in the bed at first. She described the shock of realizing that this stranger was her father, followed by strong feelings of awkwardness, self-consciousness, and a painful sense of discomfort and distance between them.

Needing to somehow bridge that distance, this woman found herself thinking of Mother Teresa's words. She writes:

> *"I never had any real relation to Christ at all, and I can't say that I did at that moment. But what came through to me was a feeling for my father's identity as . . . like a child of God. That was who he really was, behind the 'distressing disguise.' And it was my real identity too, I felt. I felt a great bond with him which wasn't anything like I'd felt as father and daughter.*
>
> *"At that point he woke up and looked at me and said, 'Hi.' And I looked at him and said, 'Hi.'*

"For the remaining months of his life we were totally at peace and comfortable together. No more self-consciousness. No unfinished business. I usually seemed to know just what was needed. I could feed him, shave him, bathe him, hold him up to fix the pillows — all these very intimate things that had been so hard for me earlier.

"In a way, this was my father's final gift to me: the chance to see him as something more than my father; the chance to see the common identity of spirit we both shared; the chance to see just how much that makes possible in the way of love and comfort. And I feel I can call on it now with anyone else."

— from Ram Dass and Paul Gorman,
How Can I Help? pp. 19–20

Forgiveness is needed only when the mask someone is wearing is not to our liking, when we have judged against it in some way. To forgive a brother is to see that he is not the mask he wears, the mask he believes to be himself. By our willingness to see Christ in him, we teach him that he has been mistaken about himself. And in offering him forgiveness, we forgive ourselves as well — for we must have mistaken our brother for his mask, and have mistaken ourselves for ours, or we never could have judged against him. All forgiveness is, at its core, self-forgiveness.

Forgiving Our Brother for What He Did Not Do

"Forgiveness recognizes what you thought your brother did to you has not occurred."

— W. p. 391; W-Pt.II.1.1:1

The Course teaches that we forgive our brother for what he did not do. Yet we have already said that forgiveness does not ask that we deny our physical senses or our physical experience in the world. So how do we understand this seeming contradiction?

Ken Wapnick has pointed out that whenever we judge someone — whether our judgment takes the form of anger, pity, worry, jealousy, contempt, or fear — we are always accusing him, in essence, of taking the peace of God away from us. We accuse him of destroying our peace of mind, destroying our sense of well-being. It is *his* fault that we are not experiencing love, safety, and joy.

Yet nothing can separate us from the experience of peace, from the love in our hearts, except our own choice, except a decision we make in our own minds. No one can take the peace of God from us. No one can destroy the perfect love in our hearts. Regardless of what our brother may have done at the level of form in the world, *he did not do this* — because he *could not* do this. What God gives is eternal as Himself. His gifts of peace and love are still within us, and we can always return to them. This is the lesson forgiveness teaches us.

The Price of Unforgiveness

We pay a heavy price for unforgiveness. We can keep a brother "guilty" only by keeping ourselves in pain, only by continuing to separate ourselves from inner peace and love.

> *"The unforgiving mind is full of fear, and offers love no room to be itself; no place where it can spread its wings in peace and soar above the turmoil of the world. The unforgiving mind is sad, without the hope of respite and release from pain. It suffers and abides in misery, peering about in darkness, seeing not, yet certain of the danger lurking there.*
>
> *"The unforgiving mind is torn with doubt, confused about itself and all it sees; afraid and angry, weak and blustering, afraid to go ahead, afraid to stay, afraid to waken or to go to sleep, afraid of every sound, yet more afraid of stillness; terrified of darkness, yet more terrified at the approach of light. What can the unforgiving mind perceive but its damnation?*
>
> *"... The unforgiving mind is in despair, without the prospect of a future which can offer anything but more despair. Yet it regards its judgment of the world as irreversible, and does not see it has condemned itself to this despair."*
>
> — W. p. 210; W-Pt.I.121.2, 3:1–2,
> 5:1–2

The unwillingness to forgive imprisons us in a nightmare of torment within our own minds. The story is told of two Hindu monks whose order forbade them to have any physical contact with women. As the two were on a journey one day, they came to a river. There an old woman pleaded with them to help her cross. One of the monks took pity on her, lifted her onto his back, carried her across to the opposite bank, and there set her down. Thanking him, she went on her way.

As the monks continued their journey, the second monk began angrily berating his companion for breaking his vows. This went on for hours. Finally the first monk, a deeply compassionate man, turned to the second and said gently, "My brother, I did carry the woman across the river. But then I set her down. You have been carrying her ever since."

One of the most graphic examples in literature of the effects of unforgiveness is the character of Miss Haversham in Charles Dickens's *Great Expectations*. Having been jilted on her wedding day, Miss Haversham stopped her life at that moment. The room in which the wedding feast was to have been held was frozen in time. The table remained set for the banquet. The room was never dusted or aired out. The curtains were kept drawn against the sunlight. Miss Haversham never wore anything but her wedding gown and never ventured outside. She lived but a grotesque parody of a life — all to bear grim witness, decade after decade, to the injury that had been done to her.

The value of such an extreme example is that we can look at it and somewhere inside ourselves say, "Enough is enough!" Despite what had happened to her, we recognize that Miss Haversham could have, at some point, decided to let it go and get on with her life. That she didn't was ultimately her own choice, and she was the one who paid the price.

In withholding forgiveness, we choose to continue living in fear, separation, and pain. In being willing to forgive, we free ourselves to return to love and to the peace of God within us. As we begin to recognize and understand clearly what we are choosing *between*, we also begin to recognize that there is only one choice that, in our hearts, we truly *want* to make.

"This ... is the time to make the easiest decision that ever confronted you, and also the only one. You will cross the bridge into reality simply because you will recognize that God is on the other side, and nothing

at all is here. It is impossible not to make the natural decision as this is realized."

— T. p. 320; T-16.V.17

Forgiveness Is Turning Within

Forgiveness is not something we *do*. It is something we *choose* and allow through our willingness to turn to the Teacher of forgiveness — the Holy Spirit — within our mind. We ask to share His perception, knowing that what He will show us will restore our minds to peace. For He will show us Christ, in our brother or sister and in ourselves. And we will cross the bridge of healing together and as one.

"As we behold that Christ in any person, in some measure at least he is healed of his humanhood and of all finite limitation, and as he beholds that in us, we, too, are lifted up.

"Enter into the sanctuary of your own being, and there in silence and secrecy behold the true identity of friend or foe. Lift up the son of God in him to your level, knowing that the Christ of him is the Christ of you."

— Joel Goldsmith,
Gift of Love, pp. 17–18

Chapter 7

The Vision of Christ

"Christ's vision is the Holy Spirit's gift, God's alternative to the illusion of separation and to the belief in the reality of sin, guilt and death. It is the one correction for all errors of perception; the reconciliation of the seeming opposites on which this world is based. Its kindly light shows all things from another point of view, reflecting the thought system that arises from knowledge and making return to God not only possible but inevitable."

— Preface: What It Says, p. xiii

A Course in Miracles is a course in changing our perception. The focus of the Course is not on *setting things right* in the world, but rather on *seeing them right.*

". . . seek not to change the world,
but choose to change your mind about the world."

— T. p. 415; T-21.Intro.1:7

However, a change of mind, a change in perception, as the Course means it, is no small thing. Nor is it a spiritual "consolation prize" we have to settle for when we seem to be powerless to bring about "real change" in the conditions we see around us. Rather it recognizes that we have the God-given power, in this and every moment, through the decision-making capacity of our own mind, to experience and reflect either hell or Heaven here on earth. And what we choose for ourselves, we offer to each other.

As we choose to look at the world with love rather than judgment, we offer it blessing instead of curse, understanding instead of blame, peace instead of attack, joy instead of pain, comfort instead of suffering. In this, the Course teaches, lies the healing and salvation of the world — and our own as well, for we receive only what we give.

Two Emotions, Two Perceptions, Two Worlds

"You have but two emotions, and one you made and one was given you. Each is a way of seeing, and different worlds arise from their different sights."

— T. pp. 232–33; T-13.V.10:1–2

The Course teaches that there are two basic emotions in our minds — fear and love. These form the basis for two entirely different ways of perceiving the world — and thus literally for experiencing two completely different worlds. The world we live in can change in an instant as we decide to shift the foundation, the premise, from which we will look at and make sense of what we see.

The Course describes and contrasts these two basic kinds of perception. "Wrong-minded perception" — the ego's way of seeing — is fear-based, arising from a premise of the reality of separation, sin, and guilt. "Right-minded" perception — the Holy Spirit's way of seeing — is love-based. Right seeing gently undoes our belief in separation, dispelling fear, restoring our minds to peace and to the awareness of love's presence.

Right-minded seeing is what the Course calls seeing with the vision of Christ. The process and practice of the Course involve recognizing when we are seeing with the ego's eyes and choosing again — choosing instead to see through the eyes of Christ. The ego sees with judgment and condemnation. Christ's vision sees with forgiveness and love. The ego sees everywhere the witnesses to guilt and to death, guilt's ultimate and inescapable punishment. The vision of Christ shows us witnesses for innocence — either innocence being expressed directly as love or else innocence that has been denied or forgotten and is calling out for our help to be recognized and remembered. These witnesses speak for the resurrection born of innocence and love that cannot die.

The ego's eyes see only the body and affirm it as our identity. The ego's sight dwells on the body's mistakes and transgressions, its shortcomings, failures, and limitations, and proclaims them our reality. Christ's vision looks past all appearances of the body to a light that shines beyond.

> *"Christ's vision has one law. It does not look upon a body, and mistake it for the Son whom God created. It beholds a light beyond the body; an idea beyond what can be touched, a purity undimmed by errors, pitiful mistakes, and fearful thoughts of guilt from dreams of sin. It sees no separation. And it looks on everyone, on every circumstance, all happenings and all events, without the slightest fading of the light it sees."*
>
> — W. p. 292; W-Pt.I.158.7

Christ's vision does not fear to look at anything in this world. It need not deny or turn away from any appearance of suffering, devastation, or pain, because it is not deceived by them. It sees with deeper sight, to *"the changeless in the heart of change; the light of truth behind appearances"* (W. p. 214; W-Pt.I.122.13:4).

Christ's vision frees us from the painful beliefs about ourselves and each other that keep us locked in dark prisons of isolation, fear, and defensiveness. It reveals to us a beauty that we rejoice to see. Our hearts open in celebration and gratitude for the love we share, a Love that shines through all creation.

The Real World

When we look upon everyone and everything in this world only through the vision of Christ, we have attained what the Course calls the "real world" — the final step before reawakening. The real world is this world seen in the light of complete forgiveness. No thought of darkness, sin, or guilt remains in our minds, concealed or projected, to hide the face of Christ from our sight.

The vision of Christ sees only Its Own reflection, the reflection of God's Love, in everything it looks upon. In this vision no one is a stranger to us, and there is nothing to fear (W. p. 296. W-Pt.I.160).

We come to this healed state of mind as we are willing to recognize first *ourselves* — our own egos, errors, and shortcomings — and then our *Self* — our real identity as wholly loved and loving sons of God — in our brothers and sisters. Remembrance of oneness begins to dawn again in our awareness, and with this comes remembrance of God.

Attainment of the real world is as far as learning can, and need, take us. When we have reached the deep and abiding peace that complete forgiveness offers us, the Course teaches, our experience will so reflect the perfect peace of Heaven that God Himself takes the final step to awaken us — much as a loving parent might gently and with great tenderness awaken a child from a peaceful sleep when morning has come.

We journey toward the real world one choice at a time. What the Course asks of us, simply and repeatedly, is that we ask for the gift of true sight, the vision of Christ, whenever we are not at peace. We need only to be willing to exchange our ego-based perceptions and judgments for those the Holy Spirit would offer us in their place.

Christ's vision is the *only* thing the Holy Spirit can give us, but that single gift contains *everything* we truly need.

> "[*Christ's vision*] *is the Holy Spirit's single gift; the treasure house to which you can appeal with perfect certainty for all the things that can contribute to your happiness. All are laid here already. All can be received but for the asking. Here the door is never locked and no one is denied his least request or his most urgent need. There is no sickness not already healed, no lack unsatisfied, no need unmet within this golden treasury of Christ.*"
>
> — W. p. 293; W-Pt.I.159.6

On this the Course is unequivocal. The *only* thing we need is right seeing — the correction of our misperceptions and our mistakes in thinking and interpretation. Everything else follows from that, naturally and organically. Our part is merely to want and choose the *miracle*, the change to right-minded perception.

How that change is accomplished and how the miracle is communicated and extended are under the direction of the Holy Spirit. The Course is clear that we need not be concerned with His part. We need only be willing to accept and fulfill our own — to let go of the judg-

ments and interpretations we have made on our own and ask to see
with the vision of Christ.

Receiving the Gift

*"[Christ] has not forgotten you. But you will not remember Him until
you look on all as He does. Who denies his brother is denying Him,
and thus refusing to accept the gift of sight by which his Self is clearly
recognized, his home remembered and salvation come."*
                                        — W. p. 296; W-Pt.I.160.10:3–5

The gift Christ's vision offers us is the healing of our own sense
of separation and the guilt and fear that follow from it. The Course
teaches again and again that our brother is a mirror in which we see
reflected who and what we believe we are.

Our perception of our brother is our perception of ourselves. Our
response to him is our response to ourselves. Our judgment of him is
the judgment we make on ourselves. What we decide he deserves is
what we offer ourselves.

*"This lesson is not difficult to learn, if you remember in your brother
you but see yourself. If he be lost in sin, so must you be; if you see light
in him, your sins have been forgiven by yourself."*
                                        — W. p. 292; W-Pt.I.158.10:3–4

The Course teaches that whatever is not love is fear, and that all
fear is a call for help, regardless of the form it takes (T. p. 200f;
T-12.I). It is this we see when we choose the vision of Christ. We
recognize that a brother's call for help simply mirrors our own, and
that the love that answers his call answers ours as well. How we answer his call is how we answer our own. We suffer together or we are
healed together.

The body's eyes see in our brother an enemy, a threat, a symbol of
separation and fear. The vision of Christ shows us the Son of God,
whose beauty and holiness and perfection is our own.

*"... in Christ's vision is [your brother's] loveliness revealed in a form
so holy and so beautiful that you could scarce refrain from kneeling at*

*his feet. Yet you will take his hand instead, for you are like him in the
sight that sees him thus."*
                                                    — W. p. 298; W-Pt.I.161.9:3–4

The Course emphasizes that every encounter we have with anyone,
even in thought, is potentially a *holy encounter* — an opportunity for
healing, a chance to see with Christ's vision instead of through the
ego's eyes of judgment and fear.

*"See no one as a body. Greet him as the Son of God he is, acknowl-
edging that he is one with you in holiness. . . .*
    *"Each brother whom you meet today provides another chance to let
Christ's vision shine on you and offer you the peace of God."*
                                                    — W. p. 292; W-Pt.I.158.8:3–4, 10:5

Asking for the Gift of Sight

*"See through the vision that is given you, for through Christ's vision
He beholds Himself. And seeing what He is, He knows His Father.
Beyond your darkest dreams He sees God's guiltless Son within you,
shining in perfect radiance that is undimmed by your dreams. And
this you will see as you look with Him, for His vision is His gift of
love to you, given Him of the Father for you."*
                                                    — T. p. 233; T-13.V.10:3–6

To see with the vision of Christ — especially in a situation that is
emotionally charged or challenging — may seem to be far beyond us,
far beyond what we are capable of. The vision of Christ certainly is
beyond our *ego* — but it is not beyond *us*. The Holy Spirit is present in
our minds. Vision is His gift to us.

Christ's vision is not something we can figure out or impose on
ourselves. It is something we can ask for, something we can be willing to accept and share. But we must want it more than we want the
ego-based perception we have already accepted. We must be willing to
"choose again."

The Voice for God within our mind gently calls to us, inviting us
to accept and share the gift of vision. We have within us a deep remembrance of beauty, a profound longing for home, a deep faith in

the possibility of healing, that will not be silenced. Somewhere in us we know there is another way. Somewhere in us we long to offer the world the peace and joy that vision offers us.

The Voice calls to us to give over the ego's "gifts" of fear-based thoughts, perceptions, and judgments, to make an open space in our minds that we may receive the gift of Christ's vision.

> " 'Choose once again' is still your only hope. Darkness cannot conceal the gifts of God unless you want it so. In peace I come, and urge you now to make an end to time and step into eternity with me. There will not be a change that eyes can see, nor will you disappear from things of time. But you will hold my hand as you return because we come together. . . . How dear are you to God, Who asks but that you walk with me and bring His light into a sickened world which fear has drained of love and life and hope.
>
> "Surely you will not fail to hear my call, for I have never failed to hear your cries of pain and grief, and I have come to save you and to redeem the world at last from fear. It never was, nor is, nor yet will be what you imagine. Let me see for you, and judge for you what you would look upon. When you have seen with me but once, you would no longer value any fearful things at cost of glory and the peace of God."
>
> — Helen Shucman, *The Gifts of God*,
> pp. 117–18

As we choose to share the vision of Christ, we become His eyes and hands and feet and voice upon the earth. There is nothing more we need to do. There is no greater gift we could offer or receive.

> "This is my offering: A quiet world, with gentle ordering and kindly thought, alive with hope and radiant in joy, without the smallest bitterness of fear upon its loveliness. Accept this now, for I have waited long to give this gift to you. I offer it in place of fear and all the 'gifts' that fear has given you. Can you choose otherwise, when all the world is standing breathless, waiting on your choice? Come now to me and we will go to God."
>
> — Helen Shucman, *The Gifts of God*,
> p. 118

Chapter 8

Come As You Are

"Come, come, whoever you are,
Wanderer, worshiper, lover of leaving —
it doesn't matter.
Ours is not a caravan of despair.
Come, even if you have broken your vow
a hundred times, ten thousand times —
Come, come again, come."

— Jelaluddin Rumi, Sufi Mystic Poet

"God takes you where you are and welcomes you."
— M. p. 62; M.26.4:10

A common pitfall for students of the Course (or other spiritual paths) is the temptation to believe that, because we are working with a path, we are now supposed to "be spiritual" — that we should be able to quickly transcend all of our ego reactions, emotions, and needs; drop all judgments; immediately forgive; let go of guilt and fear; and love everybody.

This belief sounds absurd when stated so blatantly, but it is an extremely common ego trap that can appear in sometimes subtle ways. On closer examination, it is always an expression of guilt for having an ego and trying to deny or otherwise defend against this guilt.

Ken Wapnick has pointed out that while *ultimately* the Course is a path of total ego transcendence, our immediate and ongoing work involves giving up our guilt over *having an ego*. Because it is our guilt over the ego that teaches us it must be real and reinforces our belief in and experience of separation, we cannot let go of the ego without first letting go of our guilt over it.

This guilt over having an ego can sometimes be manifest in subtle ways. It may masquerade as spiritual aspiration or even as spiritual accomplishment. We may deny even having ego reactions — like hurt, anger, emotional discomfort, fears of human closeness and intimacy, specialness desires — and we may then cloak this denial behind metaphysical rationalizations and justifications.

I once heard about a Course student who did not reach out to a friend whose father had just died, ostensibly because this student "didn't believe in death and didn't want to reinforce the belief in the illusion of death." Yet love's nature is to extend. Only the ego would ever withhold love in the face of the manifestations and illusions of the ego. Love simply sees in all expressions of ego a call for love, and naturally responds in a form that can be received without increasing fear (T. p. 20; T-2.IV.5).

To join with the peace and love of God in ourselves and from there to recognize and respond to the call for love in the grief of someone who is experiencing pain over the loss of a loved one would not be to *reinforce* the illusion of death but to *correct* it — for the content of *all* illusion is the belief that love has been destroyed or lost. To withhold love and justify our decision to withhold with metaphysical reasoning is an ego device to disguise our own fear and choice to be separate.

It is important to be clear that the distinction being made here is discerned, not at the level of behavior, but at the level of mind. The extension of love may or may not involve a physical reaching out to another. Similarly, reaching out to another can be done from a place of fear and guilt as well as from a place of love. What is needed is a willingness to be truthful with ourselves about whether we are reacting from fear, discomfort, or judgment, or genuinely responding from love. And we must recognize that any need we have to deny our own ego reactions comes from the guilt we feel over having an ego.

Having an Ego Is Not a Sin

The central premise of the ego thought system is that separation is real and that it is a sin. This translates into the idea that having an ego is a sin. We accept and express that basic belief every time we feel guilty about our ego reactions. We are released from it each time we recognize that *having an ego is not a sin*. It reflects a profoundly mistaken belief about ourselves, and it calls for correction and healing, not punishment and recrimination.

When we are willing to look at our ego reactions as our own call for love, and to respond to them with acceptance and love instead of attack and judgment, we have made the choice to let go of the ego in favor of the peace of God. Each time we make that choice we take an essential step toward the total relinquishment of the ego thought system.

One day a friend who is a Course student called me to talk about some difficulty he was having regarding a relationship. The woman he had been romantically involved with and cared about deeply had decided to seriously pursue a relationship with someone else. However, she wanted to continue having a friendship with this man, as she also genuinely cared for him and valued their relationship.

While my friend thought that he too would like to be able to continue their friendship, he was finding it painful to be with her. He recognized that he had not yet fully let go of his attachment to a romantic relationship with her. He wanted some distance, some time without seeing each other, but felt guilty about wanting and needing that. The guilt came from his recognizing clearly that the pain he was feeling was his own ego reaction and then telling himself that he should be "past that."

Essentially he was telling himself that it was not okay for him to be where he was in his own process of healing — that he "should" be more enlightened, that he should be "further along" than he was. This lack of self-acceptance is an ego device that adds insult to injury and locks us further into the experience of suffering. It expresses and reinforces a basic belief of the entire ego thought system — that there is something wrong with us, something lacking, something that needs to be changed or fixed.

Ken Wapnick has defined a good Course student as one who has come to terms with having an ego. He stresses repeatedly that we need to develop a healthy respect for the ego, for the profound degree to which we have accepted and identified with it. The undoing process that constitutes our healing can be, at times, extremely painful and terrifying to us because of this identification. And so we need to learn to meet and respond to the fear and resistance in ourselves with patience and gentleness rather than condemnation and attack.

As my friend was able to begin to look at his own ego reactions with acceptance instead of judgment, he began to experience a sense of peace and release. By forgiving himself for still having an ego, he also took an important step in transforming that particular relationship from specialness to holiness, an important step in transcending the ego.

Keep Nothing Apart

We have seen that our guilt over having an ego can express itself in outright denial of our ego reactions or in feeling guilty or ashamed for having ego reactions. Still another manifestation is taking it upon ourselves to get rid of the guilt, rather than coming in prayer to the Holy Spirit and asking for help.

For instance, in a situation in which we are upset and not at peace, we might very well recognize that we could look at things differently. We might speculate about alternative, more "enlightened" perceptions and interpretations, and then *pretend* that we already see it that way — denying how we are actually still seeing and interpreting what's going on. We might use affirmations of light to try to hide from the darkness of our actual thoughts and feelings, affirmations of wholeness to avoid facing how broken we really feel.

We need to be very clear that this is *not* the healing process of the Course. Over and over again the Course asks us to *look at* the darkness we believe is within us — both directly in our thoughts and feelings about ourselves and through the mirror of what we project onto others — and to ask the Holy Spirit to help us look at this darkness without judgment, without guilt, without fear, with His forgiveness and love.

> *"Never approach the holy instant after you have tried to remove all fear and hatred from your mind. That is its function. Never attempt to overlook your guilt before you ask the Holy Spirit's help. That is His function. Your part is only to offer Him a little willingness to let Him remove all fear and hatred, and to be forgiven."*
> — T. p. 357; T-18.V.2:1–5

I once was "told" in a meditation, "You are often very good at figuring out how something probably looks to Me. The problem is not that what you imagine is far off the mark, but rather that this keeps you from asking Me to show you what I see. It is a way of denying your need of Me, of My help. It is a subtle way of keeping Me away. And so it is a way of denying yourself, of keeping yourself from fully receiving the help and love I want to give you."

It is an ego trap to ever assume that we know what the loving or forgiving perception and response must be in a given situation confronting us. We may try to give ourselves overt or subtle rules for how we should think, feel, or act in order to be "spiritual" or "loving" people. But the real function of such rules and assumptions is to deny our need to go within and ask, situation by situation, for the guidance and help of the Teacher God has given us.

We have been told that we must "become like children" if we are to come home to Heaven. To become like a child is to acknowledge our complete dependence on our Source, who loves and cares for us and offers us all that we need for true happiness and peace. To become like a child is to be willing to reach for His hand, to ask Him in all things to lead us and show us the way.

How do we know when we need to stop and ask His help? We simply need to tell the truth about whether we are at peace. If not, we have turned away from Him — for peace is always His gift, whatever form His help may take. It doesn't matter "how much" we're not at peace. The very slightest disturbance within us means we are trying to go it alone. By trying to handle the problem ourselves, we are holding on to the problem by keeping it apart from the Answer God has placed within us.

Jesus tells us in the Course that *"we must hide nothing from each other"* (T. p. 56; T-4.III.8:2). Certainly there is nothing he would hide or withhold from us — nothing of the perfect love in his mind that he would not share with us and teach through us. We are asked in turn simply not to withhold from him — from the Holy Spirit — any of the ego thoughts that would keep our minds separate from his. We are asked only to bring to him — to bring to *light* — all our thoughts of attack, specialness, judgment, fear, vengeance, victimization, sickness, sorrow, loss, and death, all our feelings of anger, defensiveness, grief, superiority, doubt, unworthiness, terror, and pain.

He knows they are not real; we do not (T. p. 27; T-2.VII.1:3). It is his loving presence — the gentle light within our minds — that will comfort us and heal us, teaching us that these ego thoughts and feelings are not the truth of who we are. To pretend we already know that merely serves to keep his love and healing away from us, at a distance.

We can accept our need for healing without shame or guilt. Our ego thoughts and feelings are mistakes in what we believe about ourselves and nothing more. We cannot correct those mistakes ourselves, since we're the ones who made them. But we can offer our willingness to let them be corrected by bringing them to the presence of love within our minds.

The Little Willingness — "Come As You Are"

"Concentrate only on [*your willingness*], *and be not disturbed that shadows surround it. That is why you came. If you could come without them you would not need the holy instant. Come to it not in arrogance, assuming that you must achieve the state its coming brings with it. The miracle of the holy instant lies in your willingness to let it be what it is. And in your willingness for this lies also your acceptance of yourself as you were meant to be."*

— T. p. 354; T-18.IV.2:4–9

The Song of Prayer teaches that the function of prayer in this world is *reparative*. It serves a healing function, together with forgiveness, of undoing our experience of separation, guilt, and fear.

Prayer can serve this function only if we come to it truthfully, offering over the ego thoughts that are hurting us and learning that they are not met by the Holy Spirit with judgment and condemnation but are dissolved in the warmth of His acceptance and embracing love. What we keep split off from light remains in darkness to frighten us. What we offer to light becomes dissolved back into light.

At every moment, God holds out to us an invitation to "come as we are." We need not be any further along in our healing process than we are in this moment. We need not be any more "enlightened" than we are right now. We need not hide anything that we have judged shameful or unworthy in ourselves. In fact, the more willing we are to bring all of that into prayer, the more we discover that nothing we believed could separate us from God's love has the power to do that.

A friend and member of our Fellowship once shared with me a song she had written that expresses the heart of this invitation.

TELL ME

Tell me, tell me, tell me, tell me
Tell me, tell me, tell me, tell me. . . .

Tell me everything you're holding in your heart
Tell me everything you think is keeping us apart
Tell me, tell me, tell me — I'm right here

Tell me everything you're too ashamed to say
Tell me everything you think is hurting you today
Tell me, tell me, tell me, that's why I'm here
To wash away the doubts
To love away the fears

Tell me everything you think that I don't know
Tell me everything and then we'll let it go
Tell me, tell me and soon it will be clear
That you don't have to say anything
in order for me to hear

So tell me, tell me, tell me straight from your heart
and know that there is nothing
that can ever keep us apart

Tell me, tell me, tell me, tell me
Tell me, tell me, tell me — I'm right here

— Mindy Rosengarten

This is God's invitation to us all. In our willingness to come as we are — to come as we *believe* we are — we open ourselves to be shown the radiant and wondrous truth of who we *really* are. The pain we bring is exchanged for joy, the darkness we give over is dispelled by light, the valueless offerings of the ego are replaced by the shining gifts of God.

Chapter 9

Understanding "Negative" Emotions

One common misrepresentation of the Course is the idea that it teaches or encourages us to suppress or deny negative emotions. This is based on a misunderstanding and misuse of an often quoted — and indeed quite radical and uncompromising — teaching in the Course, that *"anger is never justified"* (T. p. 593; T-30.VI.1:1) Students and non-students alike sometimes take this to mean that the Course is saying that we should not get angry — or that anger is something we should feel guilty about.

Similarly, people sometimes think that the basic metaphysical teaching of the Course that this world is illusory means that the Course is telling us to go through life pretending that nothing bothers us — when in fact it does — acting as if everything that happens is okay with us — when in fact it isn't — putting up with behavior from people that inwardly we really think is terrible and forcing ourselves to smile sweetly in return. The Course is saying no such thing.

Very simply, the Course *never* asks that we deny, lie about, or minimize our subjective experience — our feelings, judgments, perceptions — to ourselves or anyone else. It never asks us to *pretend* to feel differently than we do feel. And it never tells us to feel guilty about the feelings we have. The core teaching of the Course is that healing is the *release* from guilt and fear, not the deepening of them in our minds.

Although the Course does teach metaphysically that this world is illusion, it also recognizes and states very clearly that we do not believe that. We believe that the world is real, and so it is very real for us. We are not meant to use the metaphysical teachings of the Course to pretend that we no longer take this world, or our bodies, or our ego-identities seriously. In fact we do take them very seriously — and this *is* our need for healing. We can't use metaphysical jargon or intellectual understanding to circumvent our healing process — nor does the Course in any way advocate that we do so.

How do we understand emotions — particularly painful or so-called negative emotions, in the framework of the Course? Where do they fit into the healing process? How do we work with them in our experience?

Emotions Are a Response to Perception

Although our emotional reactions always seem subjectively to be a response to something external — to something that has happened or something someone did — in fact they are always reactions to something internal, something within our own minds — to our perception and interpretation of whatever has occurred.

> *"Understand that you do not respond to anything directly, but to your interpretation of it. Your interpretation thus becomes the justification for the response."*
> — T. p. 200; T-12.I.1:4–5

Regardless of how it seems, we never react emotionally to an event or fact, but always to our perception of that event or fact — to the interpretation and meaning we give to it. The same event or action, seen in a different light or context, will have a different meaning to us — and our emotional response will be different. Our feelings are always mediated by our thoughts and interpretations, whether we are consciously aware of this process or not.

Imagine that you go into work one morning and a co-worker completely ignores your greeting to her. You feel offended and angry and think to yourself, "Who does she think *she* is?" Or, if you are a more self-blaming type, you might feel scared and upset and wonder why she's mad at you or doesn't like you. Then suppose another co-worker takes you aside and tells you that this woman's elderly father in another state had been suddenly taken ill and that the woman has been upset and preoccupied all morning.

Suddenly your feelings may be quite different. In place of the anger or personal upset you had been experiencing, you find yourself feeling sympathetic and concerned. Nothing at all has changed except your perception and understanding of the woman's behavior; you now see a call for love where before you saw an attack — and automatically your emotional response changes.

The emotions we feel are always a natural — and in that sense appropriate — response to our perception of things. If we perceive attack and blame, we will feel angry or defensive or scared. There is simply no way around that. It is a psychological reality.

> *"If you decide that someone is really trying to attack you or desert you or enslave you, you will respond as if he had actually done so, having made his error real to you.*
>
> *"... you react to your interpretations as if they were correct. You may then control your reactions behaviorally, but not emotionally. This would obviously be a split or an attack on the integrity of your mind, pitting one level within it against another."*
>
> — T. p. 200; T-12.I.1:7, 2:3–5

This passage makes very clear that merely controlling the expression of our emotional reactions is not healing. Pretending — to others or to ourselves — that we are not angry, upset, or hurt when in fact that is how we feel is not healing. Our emotions are the *result* of our perceptions. They are the symptoms of a problem, not the cause. Control or suppression at the level of symptoms is not real healing.

> *"It is pointless to believe that controlling the outcome of misthought can result in healing. When you are fearful, you have chosen wrongly. ... You must change your mind, not your behavior. ... Correction belongs only at the level where change is possible. Change does not mean anything at the symptom level, where it cannot work."*
>
> — T. p. 25; T-2.VI.3:1–2, 4, 6–7

Denying that we are feeling emotionally upset neither changes the feelings nor helps us let them go. At the same time, expressing our feelings does not, in and of itself, change them or help us let them go.

The real problem when we are upset is not at the level of what we are feeling, but at the level of how we are perceiving and giving meaning to whatever is happening. We will naturally *feel* differently when we *see* differently.

> *The only way to have a different emotional response*
> *is to have a different perception of what it happening.*

Our Perceptions — and Thus Emotions — Are a Choice We Make

A basic premise of the Course is that there are, within our minds, two basic perceptions or ways to see. We can either see through the eyes of the ego — which will always perceive separation, difference, attack, guilt, and blame — or we can see through the eyes of the Holy Spirit — which will always see wholeness, unity, innocence, the calling out of love to and for itself. At any given moment, we are choosing between these two ways to see.

By choosing between these basic perceptions, we are also choosing between two basic emotions — fear and love. The basic emotion of fear encompasses the full range of painful emotions, including anger, upset, feelings of superiority or inferiority, inadequacy, guilt, shame, depression, despair, etc. The basic emotion of love encompasses joy, well-being, connectedness, and peace.

The Course asks us to work with the idea that we *choose* which perception — and thus which emotion — we will have — even though we do not usually experience making that choice consciously. Our subjective experience is that we are seeing and reacting to what is "out there." It certainly does seem that way — but we can also recognize and appreciate that things are not always what they seem.

For instance, have you ever noticed that there are some days when things that usually "get to you" simply don't? And that there are other days when things that normally don't bother you seem to set you off? Think about that more closely for a moment. If you can have different reactions to the same events, then the events cannot be the cause of your reactions. Something in you must account for the differences in how you react. According to the Course, that "something" is the inner choice we make between seeing with the ego and seeing with the Holy Spirit. And the result of that choice will be the experience of either some kind of upset and turmoil, or peace.

When the Course says that anger is never justified, it is reminding us that the source of our anger is not outside of us, but inside — not in what is happening but in how we are perceiving and interpreting what is happening. In truth we are not *reactive* but *pro-active*. We choose the emotional experience we will have by choosing which perception we will accept — that of the ego or that of the Holy Spirit. Anger always reflects that we have chosen to identify with the ego.

Our Emotions Show Us
Which Choice We've Made

From the perspective of the Course, then, our emotions are signals to us of which choice we've made. If we are feeling angry, upset, anxious, depressed, guilty, or frightened, — we have already chosen to identify with the ego, with the ego's belief in and perception of separation, guilt, and attack. Knowing that does not necessarily make the pain of those emotions any less, nor does it necessarily mean we are ready to make a different choice. Knowing that simply points us in the direction of where our healing and release can be found when we are ready and willing to receive healing.

The Course teaches that we need not be victims of our painful emotions. We are not "stuck" with them, nor does the world have to change for us to be able to let them go. There is always another choice we can make, another way for us to see, in any situation that seems to be a source of pain. We can always ask the Holy Spirit for a perception that will replace fear, whatever its form, with love. Love answers our call with the experience of peace.

This other perception, the loving perception that brings us peace, is not something we can figure out ourselves or come up with on our own. Rather it is "given" to us by the Holy Spirit when we are honestly willing to let it replace our own. This is what the Course refers to as the *miracle*, or *forgiveness*. It is a perception that is, in fact, already present in our minds. It is the way we naturally see things when we are "in our right mind," when we are aware of and experiencing our connection with love, with God.

In true forgiveness we do not try to force ourselves to feel loving and open-hearted toward someone whom we inwardly continue to fear or resent. Forgiveness has occurred when we literally see the person and see what happened differently — when we see in such a way that our natural feeling response is one of peace, connection, and love, for one whom we recognize as our brother or sister, a beloved child of our Father.

Negative Emotions Are Not a Sin

The Course makes clear that feelings of anger, depression, hatefulness, and fear are the inevitable consequence of accepting the belief in separation, of buying the ego's bill of goods and choosing the ego in place of God. Because everyone in this world has done that, those feelings are a part of everyone's life experience and journey of healing.

It is so easy for students of the Course to fall into the trap of thinking that choosing for the ego is a sin. If this were so, it would follow that feeling negative emotions would also be a sin — which would mean we should feel guilty about feeling angry, hateful, depressed, or afraid. This in turn would lead to being afraid of these feelings and would reinforce our need to defend against them through suppression, denial, or projection. Employing these defenses serves only to delay the process of correcting the faulty perceptions and beliefs in our minds that gave rise to these emotions in the first place.

It cannot be stated too emphatically or too often that this is *not* what the Course teaches. In fact, this very way of thinking is the basic mistake the Course seeks to help us correct. We need to remember that *only the ego would condemn our choosing to side with the ego* — because only the ego condemns anything. The Holy Spirit does not condemn. The Holy Spirit sees our choice of the ego's way of seeing as a mistake, not a sin — and sees all mistakes as calls for love (T. p. 200; T-12.I).

We need not feel guilty about our feelings of anger, fear, depression, or hate. We do need to be willing to see them as our own call for love — as a sign that we have temporarily lost sight of our connection with God, temporarily forgotten the perfect love within us that is our true nature and the perfect peace that is our inheritance.

The Question of Expression

A question that often arises with respect to "negative" emotions is whether or not we should express our upset feelings to the person they seem to be directed toward. There are widely varying theories and opinions, both in psychology and folk wisdom, concerning the value of expressing anger. What would be the perspective of the Course?

The Course asks us to think of everything in this world of form as *neutral*. The only question it makes sense to ask of anything in the world, the Course teaches, is *"What is it for, what is its purpose?"* (T. p. 61; T-4.V.6) The meaning or value of anything depends entirely on the purpose we choose for it, on whether we give it over to the ego or to the Holy Spirit to use. Whatever is placed in the hands of the ego will further reinforce our experience of separation, guilt, and fear. Whatever is given over to the Holy Spirit will serve healing.

Behavior is a part of the world of form, and expressing emotion is behavior. It can serve either the purpose of attack — the ego's basic purpose — or the purpose of communication — the Holy Spirit's sole function. Thus from the standpoint of the Course, there can be no rule about whether or not we should express our emotions in a given situation — because it is not the behavior itself, but the purpose of the behavior that matters.

We all know from experience that sometimes the expression of painful emotions serves only to reinforce and strengthen those emotions in us. Other times expressing our emotions is a helpful and essential step in letting them go. Our job is not to decide on our own what is right to do. Our job is merely to decide between serving the ego and serving the Holy Spirit. Looking for rules for behavior — such as it is always good to express our upset to the person involved, or it is never helpful to express our anger directly — is most often an ego device to prevent us from turning to the Holy Spirit to guide us situation by situation. If we think we already know what to do, we will not bother to ask for His direction.

When we are upset, we certainly need to be truthful with ourselves about what we are feeling. We need to recognize that we are upset because we have already sided with our ego and that we need to join with the Holy Spirit if we want to regain inner peace. We need to bring our feelings and thoughts to the Holy Spirit, to be willing to look at them with neither judgment nor justification. We need to ask for healing and help, for a miracle, for another way to see. And then we do whatever seems right to do, trusting that the Holy Spirit will direct us toward healing of all concerned and trusting that if we do make a wrong choice of action the Holy Spirit will help us recognize our mistake and correct it.

All healing, the Course teaches, is release from fear and guilt. People who have been afraid of their feelings may well need to learn that they can get angry or upset and that God will not abandon or punish them. Getting in touch with negative feelings and expressing them can be a necessary and important step in our healing process — not for its own sake, not to glorify or increase our investment in these feelings, but because it is essential to learn that our ego thoughts and emotions do not destroy God's love for and in us. They simply block God's love and peace from our awareness at a given moment because we cannot hold two opposing perceptions simultaneously. But the loving, healing perception of the Holy Spirit remains available to us as an alternative — always. And the joy and peace of God remain but a choice away.

Healing Our Pain

In a practical sense, there may be lots of times on our healing journey, in the course of a day, when we are able to work with this approach to our upsets and fairly easily make a different choice. Yet there are also experiences and challenges that seem much greater, that strike closer to the core of our ego identifications and attachments, where the prospect of changing our minds and letting go of the painful perceptions seems much more difficult. In these situations our subjective experience is often like peeling an onion. We release one layer of pain or anger or grief only to find another waiting below.

We have, in fact, developed layer upon layer of defenses to keep the core of the ego thought system intact. And our healing experience, even in a given situation, may seem to move through these layers. The essential thing from the standpoint of the Course is simply to remember that the basic principles of healing remain the same, whether the situation is a tiny slight or a profound loss at the level of the world.

The Course teaches that fear brought to love will always yield to love. All of our painful emotions are expressions of fear, whatever outer form they seem to take. And only love can heal them by correcting them at their source. Little by little we bring our pain to the Comforter given us, and little by little we let His unconditional acceptance and love — rather than our own efforts at manipulation and control — work the healing in us. Weeping may endure for the ego's night, but joy comes with God's dawning.

Chapter 10

"Rules for Decision"

Part 1

"This is not a course in the play of ideas,
but in their practical application."

— T. p. 196; T-11.VIII.5:3

The Course describes itself as a course in *"mind training"* (T. p. 13; T-1.VII.4:1). Repeatedly it stresses that it is a practical course. Like Buddha — who wanted, not to engage in abstract theological debate, but to offer practical teaching to help alleviate the suffering in this world — the Course is most immediately concerned with our healing and release from the deep pain and fear that characterize so much of our experience.

Ken Wapnick points out that the theology and metaphysics of the Course provide the foundation that makes our complete healing and awakening not only possible but inevitable. But the Course also tells us clearly that the real nature of God, of Heaven, of our true Self is far beyond what is possible for us to comprehend with a mind that is split. And so the focus and "work" of the Course lie in our applying its teachings within our experience here — practicing forgiveness, learning to choose more consistently to align in purpose and perception with the Holy Spirit, allowing our split mind to be healed and unified.

Near the end of the Text is a section entitled "Rules for Decision," which outlines a step-by-step process by which we can develop the habit of applying the ideas that can *"lead [us] from dreams of judgment to forgiving dreams and out of pain and fear"* (T. p. 581; T-30.Intro.1:5).

It offers a simple set of guidelines and practice that translates the theory of the Course into a basic and natural guidance for how we think and live.

We can look at this section of the Text in some detail as a way of understanding and deepening our appreciation of the practical nature and process of the Course.

> "*Decisions are continuous. You do not always know when you are making them. But with a little practice with the ones you recognize, a set begins to form which sees you through the rest. It is not wise to let yourself become preoccupied with every step you take. The proper set, adopted consciously each time you wake, will put you well ahead.*"
> — T. p. 581; T-30.I.1:1–5

This paragraph is very similar in tone to the general guidelines offered near the end of the Manual for Teachers.

> "*To ask the Holy Spirit to decide for you is simply to accept your true inheritance. Does this mean that you cannot say anything without consulting Him? No, indeed! That would hardly be practical, and it is the practical with which this course is most concerned. If you have made it a habit to ask for help when and where you can, you can be confident that wisdom will be given you when you need it. Prepare for this each morning, remember God when you can throughout the day, ask the Holy Spirit's help when it is feasible to do so, and thank Him for His guidance at night. And your confidence will be well founded indeed.*"
> — M. p. 68; M-29.5:4–10

Both of these passages suggest that

1. we will gradually assimilate the principles and teachings of this path (and receive the healing they offer us) if we are willing to make use of them when and as we can, and

2. we can best do that if we start each day by consciously establishing the right frame of mind.

The ego often tries to sabotage our learning and perseverance by insisting that we have to be perfect in our practice in order to make any real progress along the spiritual path. But the Course points out more than once that *"readiness... is not mastery"* (M. p. 14; M.4.IX.1:10). Each small step we take in the right direction contributes to the whole and is worthwhile.

A valuable model for how to think about our practice is provided in the first few lessons of the Workbook. We are not asked in those lessons to try to apply the idea to absolutely everything. Rather we are asked to not purposely or specifically *exclude* anything from its application.

It is not helpful to become obsessed with being inclusive. Obsession is a defense against, and thus an expression of, guilt and fear. An increase in fear and guilt is the opposite of healing, a deeper immersion in the ego's craziness and pain. This is *never* what the Course is advocating.

What is helpful and necessary is to be truthful with ourselves about any unwillingness or resistance we have to being inclusive. We need to be honest about the times we want to exclude a particular person or situation from the application of the Course's teachings — when, for instance, our mind says that yes, forgiveness is always the answer, *except* in *this* situation or with *that* person.

Similarly, we need not become obsessed or preoccupied with consulting the Holy Spirit about every decision we have to make in the course of a day. But we do need to be truthful about which decisions we specifically do *not* want to ask Him about, which ones we want to exclude Him from.

> *"... if you find resistance strong and dedication weak, you are not ready. Do not fight yourself. But think about the kind of day you want, and tell yourself there is a way in which this very day can happen just like that. Then try again to have the day you want."*
> — T. p. 581; T-30.I.1:6–9

The healing process of the Course is a very gentle, gradual process. There are some systems of growth or healing that advocate breaking down or pushing through resistance. The Course is not one of these. Resistance is an expression of fear. Fighting against our fear increases our defensiveness, which reinforces the fear and makes it more real in our minds. We are asked instead to recognize in our fear — in our resistance — our own call for love. Love is patient, kind, accepting. In its gentle light fear gradually melts away — like ice in the sun's warmth. As fear dissolves, we naturally become ready to take our next step.

Rather than fight ourselves if we find we are resistant, the Course suggests that we ask ourselves what kind of day we want to have. Here the Course is referring to the *content* of the day, not the *form*. This can be a day of happiness, serenity, and perfect peace, if that is what I want. The "rules for decision" provide the framework for me to have that kind of day.

> *"(1) The outlook starts with this:*
>
> **Today I will make no decisions by myself...**
>
> *"(2) Throughout the day, at any time you think of it and have a quiet moment for reflection, tell yourself again the kind of day you want; the feelings you would have, the things you want to happen to you, and the things you would experience, and say:*
>
> **If I make no decisions by myself,**
> **this is the day that will be given me.**
>
> *"These two procedures, practiced well, will serve to let you be directed without fear, for opposition will not first arise and then become a problem in itself."*
>
> — T. pp. 581, 582; T-30.I.2:1–2;4:1–3

We are asked to start by deciding that we will make no decisions today without the Holy Spirit's guidance, perspective, and help, and to remind ourselves of that basic choice from time to time throughout the day.

The emphasis on asking the Holy Spirit's help and guidance in all our decisions can be found throughout the Course. We are told that we cannot make any sane decisions without His help, nor is it necessary to make any decisions without Him.

> *"Whenever you choose to make decisions for yourself*
> *you are thinking destructively,*
> *and the decision will be wrong."*
>
> — T. p. 256; T-14.III.9:1

"It will never happen
that you must make decisions for yourself.
You are not bereft of help,
and Help that knows the answer."

— T. p. 257; T-14.III.11:1–2

Although within the world there appear to be many decisions that
we need to make, in fact, the Course tells us, there is really just one.
But it is one that is being made in every moment. It is a decision with
only two fixed alternatives, no matter how diverse the forms these alternatives may appear to take. It is the decision whether to look out
upon the world from our wrong-mind or from our right-mind, to
think with the ego or the with Holy Spirit, to come from fear or from
love.

"Each day, each hour and minute, even every second, you are deciding
between the crucifixion and the resurrection, between the ego and the
Holy Spirit. The ego is the choice for guilt; the Holy Spirit the choice
for guiltlessness. The power of decision is all that is yours. What you
can decide between is fixed, because there are no alternatives except
truth and illusion. And there is no overlap between them, because
they are opposites which cannot be reconciled and cannot both be true.
You are guilty or guiltless, bound or free, unhappy or happy."
— T. p. 255; T-14.III.4

Although the decisions we believe we need to make here within the
world of form are all — from a metaphysical perspective — simply part
of the illusion, as long as we still believe this world is real that is not a
lesson we yet have mastered. We are not asked to start beyond the level
of our perceived need. But we are asked to recognize that we need the
help of a Guide who will use our decision-making to lead us out of
illusion instead of deeper into it.

"You have been told to ask the Holy Spirit for the answer to any
specific problem, and that you will receive a specific answer if such is
your need. You have also been told that there is only one problem and
one answer. In prayer this is not contradictory. There are decisions to
make here, and they must be made whether they be illusions or not.

*You cannot be asked to accept answers which are beyond the level of
need you can recognize. Therefore, it is not the form of the question
that matters, nor how it is asked. The form of the answer, if given by
God, will suit your need as you see it."*
— SOP. p. 2; SOP-1.I.2:1–7

All decisions we make in this world stem from how we judge,
interpret, and make sense of the "facts" of a situation. We take an
important step when we realize that the only decision we can make
is whether to accept the ego's meaning and interpretation of the situation or those of the Holy Spirit. In any decision-making situation
facing us, we will accept one or the other and then "decide" what to
do accordingly.

The first rule for decision, then — that I will make no decisions
myself today — is merely a statement of a simple fact: that I *cannot*
make any decisions myself. I will make all of them either with the ego
or with the Holy Spirit. The first rule is thus really a statement of a
deeper decision to identify with the Holy Spirit rather than with the
ego in how I look at, define, and perceive all that happens today.

*"We said you can begin a happy day with the determination not to
make decisions by yourself. This seems to be a real decision in itself.
And yet, you **cannot** make decisions by yourself. The only question
really is with what you choose to make them. That is really all. The
first rule, then, is not coercion, but a simple statement of a simple fact.
You will not make decisions by yourself whatever you decide. For they
are made with idols or with God. And you ask help of anti-Christ or
Christ, and which you choose will join with you and tell you what
to do."*
— T. p. 584; T-30.I.14

Peace, happiness, and calm certainty can be ours throughout the
day — whatever may arise and require a response from us — if we will
ask the Holy Spirit to be the eyes with which we see and the mind
with which we understand and define what is happening. His perception and perspective will automatically guide us in the best and most
helpful course of action for ourselves and everyone else concerned in
each situation. We need only to ask His help to see clearly and rightly.

This sounds so simple, and in truth it is. And yet our experience is very often quite different from this. Our experience of asking the Holy Spirit's guidance and help may frequently be fraught with conflict, fear, or frustration. What's going on?

> *"This is your major problem now. You still make up your mind, and then decide to ask what you should do. And what you hear may not resolve the problem as you saw it first. This leads to fear, because it contradicts what you perceive and so you feel attacked. And therefore angry. There are rules by which this will not happen. But it does occur at first, while you are learning how to hear."*
>
> — T. pp. 581–82; T-30.I.3

We run into problems in our asking when we have already aligned and identified with our ego in defining the situation and judging what we think is the best solution. We are not really asking then with an open mind. Either we will not hear the Holy Spirit's answer at all, or we will be angry, fearful, and resistant to what we hear.

The Course offers us a clear process by which this conflict can be undone and we can be restored to inner peace. We'll examine this process in detail in the next chapter.

Chapter 11

"Rules for Decision"

Part 2

"...ask the Holy Spirit everything, and leave all decisions to His gentle counsel....

"Let Him... be your only Guide that you would follow to salvation. He knows the way, and leads you gladly on it. With Him you will not fail to learn that what God wills for you is your will. Without His guidance you will think you know alone, and will decide against your peace...."

— T. pp. 257, 258; T-14.III.12:6, 14:1–4

"Say to the Holy Spirit only, 'Decide for me,' and it is done."

— T. p. 258; T-14.III.16:1

The Course teaches that every day can be a day of perfect happiness, serenity, and well-being if we are willing to turn all of our decisions over to the Holy Spirit's guidance. By inviting Him to direct our thinking and perception in all that we encounter, we learn through Him that God's Will for us is the deep joy, changeless love, and abiding peace we so long for in our hearts as well.

We are asked to begin our day by making a basic choice to decide nothing for ourselves today, but to ask His direction in all things. In establishing this mind-set, we accept that not only will we not, without the Holy Spirit's guidance, judge what to do in situations where we are called on to respond, but also that we will not judge the situations themselves.

To judge something is to define what it is and what it is for. As soon as we judge or define for ourselves what a situation is, we have given it a meaning. We have framed the nature of the problem in a particular way, and thereby have also framed what an appropriate response must be. Once we have decided what the problem is, we are no longer open-minded in asking the Holy Spirit's guidance.

In such a situation we may feel a resistance to, or fear of, asking. We have already decided what we want the answer to be. We may then simply "forget" to ask. We may go through the motions of asking and experience not getting an answer at all — because we are closed and unwilling to hear anything but the ego's voice.

If we do ask and receive an answer different from what we're looking for, we are likely to be frightened, confused, angry, disturbed. We are likely to feel we are being asked to do something against our own desires and self-interest. We may feel coerced, misunderstood, violated, and attacked. We become caught up, in our minds, defending and justifying our position, increasingly invested in being "right" — despite the heavy cost to our inner peace.

Returning to Open Mind

"Whenever you think you know, peace will depart from you, because you have abandoned the Teacher of peace. Whenever you fully realize that you know not, peace will return, for you will have invited Him to do so by abandoning the ego on behalf of Him. Call not upon the ego for anything; it is only this that you need do. The Holy Spirit will, of Himself, fill every mind that so makes room for Him."
— T. p. 278; T-14.XI.13:3–6

We are all still on the journey of healing. We are all still "works in progress." We all still operate with a mind that is split. We are all still called by two voices and often choose to listen to the ego. And so — even when we begin our day by deciding that we will make no decisions without the Holy Spirit — we find at times that we have already decided on our own. To decide on our own is to decide with the ego.

The Course is very specific about what to do when we find ourselves there. If we can catch the process early on — if we notice any resistance in ourselves to asking the Holy Spirit's direction in a particular situation — we must recognize that we have already defined the situation for ourselves. We think we know what the situation means, what the problem or question is and what the answer should be. Our real need at that point is to return to what in Zen is called "beginner's mind" — a place of open-mindedness, a recognition that we do not know.

We need to recognize that any judgment we have made without the Holy Spirit has been made with our ego. It must therefore be based on a limited, fragmented perspective that is also past-referential. Such a perception must interfere with our ability to see clearly what is really going on in this moment and will inevitably mislead us. We must decide that this is *not* what we truly want.

Yet, again, before we can make that decision we have to recognize that we are indeed walking the wrong road. How do we know if this is the case?

The Course is very clear and specific about what we are to use as our guideline in this. We are asked to look honestly at our inner experience.

"*How can you know whether you chose the stairs to Heaven or the way to hell? Quite easily. How do you feel? Is peace in your awareness? Are you certain which way to go? And are you sure the goal of Heaven can be reached? If not, you walk alone. Ask, then, your Friend to join with you, and give you certainty of where you go.*"
— T. p. 460; T-23.II.22:6–13

Simply, if we feel any reluctance or resistance to asking the Holy Spirit's direction and help in a given decision, we have judged already. Resistance is a sign that inner conflict exists — and any conflict, even seemingly slight, is lack of peace. It is a sure-fire signal that our ego is already involved and guiding us.

We are asked then to remember the kind of day we want — a day

of happiness and peace — and to remember Who can guide us to that
kind of day.

> *"Remember once again the day you want, and recognize that some-*
> *thing has occurred that is not part of it. Then realize that you have*
> *asked a question by yourself, and must have set an answer in your*
> *terms. Then say,*
>
> > *'I have no question. I forgot what to decide.'*
>
> *"This cancels out the terms that you have set, and lets the answer show*
> *you what the question must have really been."*
>
> — T. p. 582; T-3.I.6

This process is very similar to what is suggested in a section of the
Text entitled "The Test of Truth."

> *"When your peace is threatened or disturbed in any way, say to*
> *yourself,*
>
> > *'I do not know what anything, including this, means.*
> > *And so I do not know how to respond to it.*
> > *And I will not use my own past learning as the light to guide*
> > *me now.'*
>
> *"By this refusal to attempt to teach yourself what you do not know,*
> *the Guide Whom God has given you will speak to you. He will take*
> *His rightful place in your awareness the instant you abandon it, and*
> *offer it to Him."*
>
> — T. p. 277; T-14.XI.6:6–11

A friend of mine once observed, "A true question is innocent of its
answer." If we can return to open-mindedness — if we are willing to
recognize and let go of the definition and meaning we have placed on
the situation — we will once again be able to ask a true question and be
receptive to the Holy Spirit's answer. And we will be open to learning
again, more deeply, that His answer will always bring us peace.

We are encouraged to return to this state of mind as quickly as
possible. Otherwise, our investment in our own point of view — in the
question as we have framed it and the answer we think will bring us
happiness —

"... will gain momentum, until you believe the day you want is one in which you get your answer to your question. And you will not get it, for it would destroy the day by robbing you of what you really want. This can be very hard to realize, when once you have decided by yourself the rules that promise you a happy day. Yet this decision still can be undone, by simple methods you can accept."

— T. p. 582; T-30.I.7:3–6

Often we do not seem to catch ourselves in this process until we are already heavily invested in the answer we think we want, already heavily invested in being right. We then are faced with what the Course poses as a very basic question:

"Do you prefer that you be right or happy?"

— T. p. 573; T-29.VII.1:9

In our confusion we have come to believe that our happiness depends on being right. We need to be gently guided through a process that undoes this mistake in our thinking and redirects us to where our happiness can, in truth, be found — in God's Will for us. We need to be gently guided to the discovery that God's Will for us is not in opposition to ours, but is our own, and is our happiness.

We'll look next at the step-by-step process described in the Course that can lead us out of these deeper places of confusion and opposition to asking for guidance and help.

Chapter 12

"Rules for Decision"

Part 3

"The Holy Spirit is your Guide in choosing. He is in the part of your mind that always speaks for the right choice, because He speaks for God. He is your remaining communication with God, which you can interrupt but cannot destroy. The Holy Spirit is the way in which God's Will is done on earth as it is in Heaven. Both Heaven and earth are in you, because the call of both is in your mind. . . . Your divided devotion has given you the two voices, and you must choose at which altar you want to serve. . . . The decision is very simple. It is made on the basis of which call is worth more to you."
— T. p. 70; T-5.II.8:1–5, 9, 11–12

"Every decision you make is for Heaven or for hell, and brings you the awareness of what you decided for."
— T. p. 286; T-15.III.5:7

As we practice following a spiritual path like the Course, we learn increasingly to turn to the Holy Spirit, or Inner Teacher, for direction in all decisions and situations we face. We begin to understand that we make *every* decision either with the Holy Spirit or with the ego — and that who we decide *with* determines our experience of the situation and the decision.

The Course teaches that we can establish a general mind-set of turning all decisions over to the Holy Spirit. We can begin each day with the goal that this be a day of serenity and happiness — recognizing that this is also God's Will for us — and accept that we can have such a day if we will make all our decisions with the Holy Spirit's guidance and help.

Yet it is also clear that sometimes we decide with the ego — that is, we judge and define a problem or situation for ourselves — before we even realize this has occurred. We can recognize that this must be the case, however, if we find ourselves resisting the Holy Spirit's help, reluctant to ask, fearful of, or upset about, receiving an answer that contradicts our own thoughts or wishes.

If we can catch this dynamic early — before our investment in our ego-based viewpoint has gained momentum and solidified — we can return without much difficulty to the openness of mind needed to ask the Holy Spirit's guidance and receive His answer with gladness and peace. We simply need to acknowledge what has happened, to remember that on our own we do not know how to judge and give meaning to the situation, and to recognize that we do, in fact, need and want His guidance and help.

There are times, though, that we do become strongly invested in our way of looking at the situation and in receiving the answer we think we want. At such times we find ourselves feeling conflicted, anxious, angry, self-righteous, confused, upset. We are defensive about our point of view, entrenched in thinking that our welfare depends on our being right. We do not want the Holy Spirit's answer, believing it would require some kind of sacrifice or loss on our part.

From such a position, to return to a true openness in our minds and hearts — an openness to receive God's love and help — requires a process of gentle and gradual undoing of our sense of opposition and fear. It is this process we'll now focus on.

The Process of Undoing

The steps of this undoing process are simple and clear. They are needed whenever we feel ourselves deeply in conflict or feel a strong sense of opposition to wholeheartedly asking the Holy Spirit to decide for us — to asking to see as He sees or to turning our thinking and responding completely over to Him.

The Course never asks us to be dishonest about where we are in our process. We are never asked to be untruthful about our own thoughts and feelings, with ourselves or with the Holy Spirit. We are never asked to pretend that we want His counsel while we still fear it. Instead we are guided gently through a series of steps in which we discover that we in fact *do* want His answer, and not our own.

When we find ourselves unwilling or unable to let go of our definition of a problem or situation, we are asked instead to start by simply being truthful about whether or not we like what we are feeling — the anxiety, anger, confusion, conflict, tension, defensiveness, upset, fear we are experiencing.

> *"If you are so unwilling to receive you cannot even let your question go, you can begin to change your mind with this:*
>
> ### *'At least I can decide I do not like what I feel now.'*
>
> *"This much is obvious, and paves the way for the next easy step."*
> — T. pp. 582–83; T-30.I.8

There is a saying in Twelve Step recovery programs: "My own best thinking got me to where I am." The next step in the undoing process requires our willingness to acknowledge that there is a relationship between the feelings we're feeling and the way we've been thinking about and interpreting the situation. We need to recognize that the price tag attached to our being "right" in our thinking is the painful way we are feeling.

> *"Having decided that you do not like the way you feel, what could be easier than to continue with,*
>
> ### *'And so I hope I have been wrong.'*
>
> *"This works against the sense of opposition, and reminds you that help is not being thrust upon you but is something that you want and that you need, because you do not like the way you feel. This tiny opening will be enough to let you go ahead....*
>
> *"Now you have reached the turning point, because it has occurred to you that you will gain if what you have decided is not so. Until this point is reached, you will believe your happiness depends on being*

right. But this much reason have you now attained; you would be better off if you were wrong."
− T. p. 583; T-30.I.9, 10

Once we have decided that we don't like how we feel and that we would like to feel better — and that our feelings are the result of how we have been looking at and defining the situation — the next step is obvious. If we want to feel better, we need a different point of view on things, a different perception.

"This tiny grain of wisdom will suffice to take you further. You are not coerced, but merely hope to get a thing you want. And you can say in perfect honesty,

'I want another way to look at this.'

"Now you have changed your mind about the day, and have remembered what you really want. Its purpose has no longer been obscured by the insane belief that you want it for the goal of being right when you are wrong. Thus is readiness for asking brought to your awareness, for you cannot be in conflict when you ask for what you want, and see that it is this for which you ask."
− T. p. 583; T-30.I.11

At this point we begin honestly to want the Holy Spirit's perception in place of the ego's, because we remember that we want peace more than we want to be right. We are ready to ask the Teacher of peace to show us the way to peace. For what He offers us we recognize as what we truly want.

"This final step is but acknowledgment of lack of opposition to be helped. It is a statement of open mind, not certain yet, but willing to be shown.

'Perhaps there is another way to look at this.
What can I lose by asking?'

"Thus you now can ask a question that makes sense, and so the answer will make sense as well. Nor will you fight against it, for you see that it is you who will be helped by it."
− T. p. 583; T-30.I.12

With this we have returned to the place in our minds where we naturally want to align with the Holy Spirit's perception of and purpose for every situation and event in our lives. And in our simple desire for that alignment it is accomplished in us. We need but wait for it to be revealed. And it will be, in a way we can recognize and understand.

It is important that we not feel guilty about having to go through this undoing process. We have simply made the wrong decision — the decision to see and think with the ego. All the many specific forms this wrong decision can take are mistakes that can be corrected, if we are willing to look at them and not hold onto them. We are not asked to be perfect — only willing to practice what we are being taught.

> *"It must be clear that it is easier to have a happy day if you prevent unhappiness from entering at all. But this takes practice in the rules that will protect you from the ravages of fear. When this has been achieved, the sorry dream of judgment has forever been undone. But meanwhile, you have need for practicing the rules of undoing."*
>
> — T. pp. 583–84; T-30.I.13:1–4

The Decision for God

A similar process of undoing is described in the section of the Text entitled "The Decision for God."

> *"Decision cannot be difficult. This is obvious, if you realize that you must already have decided not to be wholly joyous if that is how you feel. Therefore, the first step in the undoing is to recognize that you actively decided wrongly, but can as actively decide otherwise. Be very firm with yourself in this, and keep yourself fully aware that the undoing process, which does not come from you, is nevertheless within you because God placed it there. Your part is merely to return your thinking to the point at which the error was made, and give it over to the Atonement in peace. Say this to yourself as sincerely as you can,*

remembering that the Holy Spirit will respond fully to your slightest invitation:

> *'I must have decided wrongly, because I am not at peace.*
> *I made the decision myself, but I can also decide otherwise.*
> *I want to decide otherwise, because I want to be at peace.*
> *I do not feel guilty, because the Holy Spirit will undo all the*
>   *consequences of my wrong decision if I will let Him.*
> *I choose to let Him, by allowing Him to decide for God for*
>   *me.'"*

— T. p. 83; T-5.VII.6

To decide for God is to decide for God in us — for our real Self. To follow the guidance of the Holy Spirit is to follow the deepest longing of our own true nature — to follow the path of our heart that wants only to open in love.

> *"Every decision you make stems from what you think you are, and represents the value you put on yourself."*

— T. p. 285; T-15.III.3:3

In every decision we make, we reinforce how we see ourselves — as children of God or children of the ego. We will see our own best interest either as unified with everyone's or as separate and opposing. What we choose determines what we experience — peace or war — and what we teach and offer to our brothers and sisters.

We make *every* decision with either the ego or the Holy Spirit. We offer *every* moment to one or the other. And we offer to the world what we accept for ourselves. Not only can we make no decisions *by* ourselves, we can make no decisions *for ourselves alone.*

> *"I am alone in nothing.*
> *Everything I think or say or do*
> *teaches all the universe."*

— W. p. 87; W-Pt.I.R.I.54.4:2

"It is not true that you can make decisions by yourself or for yourself alone. No thought of God's Son can be separate or isolated in its effects.

Every decision is made for the whole Sonship, directed in and out, and influencing a constellation larger than anything you ever dreamed of."
                                        — T. p. 257; T-14.III.9:3–5

We cannot possibly know with our limited ego mind what is best for everyone touched in any way by a situation confronting us. To ask the Holy Spirit to decide for us is to ask only that love's blessing be extended to all. We need not comprehend what the full outworking of love will be. Love knows its own way. We need only choose if we are willing to let it flow through us, today, in this moment, in this situation.

"How gracious it is to decide all things through Him Whose equal Love is given equally to all alike!...In everything be led by Him, and do not reconsider. Trust Him to answer quickly, surely, and with Love for everyone who will be touched in any way by the decision. And everyone will be."
                                        — T. p. 258; T-14.III.17:1, 4–6

Your Day Is Your Gift to the World

How we choose to go through our day, the way we choose to make decisions — with the ego or with the Holy Spirit — is our offering to the world.

"Your day is not at random. It is set by what you choose to live it with, and how the friend whose counsel you have sought perceives your happiness....

"The day you want you offer to the world, for it will be what you have asked for, and will reinforce the rule of your adviser in the world."
                                        — T. p. 584; T-30.I.15:1–2, 16:7

As we practice the rules for decision and align ourselves more and more with the Holy Spirit's guidance, we gift not only ourselves but everyone.

Ask yourself this one question each morning:

"Whose kingdom is the world for you today?
What kind of day will you decide to have?"

— T. p. 584; T-30.I.16:8–9

And remember — you answer not for yourself alone, but for all the world along with you. The world waits for you, for me, for each of us, to answer with love.

Chapter 13

"I Will Be with You"

Accepting Our Part in God's Plan

"And God said, 'I have seen the miserable state of my people in Egypt. I have heard their appeal to be free. . . . I am aware of their sufferings. I mean to deliver them out of the hands of the Egyptians and bring them out of that land to a land rich and broad, a land where milk and honey flow. . . . The cry of the sons of Israel has come unto me. . . . So come, I send you to Pharaoh to bring the sons of Israel, my people, out of Egypt.'

"But Moses said to God, 'Who am I that I should go to Pharaoh and bring the sons of Israel out of Egypt?'

"And God answered, 'I will be with You.'"

— Exodus 3:7–12

"Can you to whom God says, 'Release my Son!' be tempted not to listen, when you learn that it is you for whom He asks release? And what but this is what this course would teach? And what but this is there for you to learn?"

— T p. 619; T-31.VII.15:6–7

When God revealed Himself to Moses in the burning bush and told Moses that he was to lead the Israelites out of their bondage into freedom, Moses' immediate, automatic response was, *"Who am I to do this? I'm nobody!"* And God reassured him, simply, *"I will be with you."*

There are times in each of our lives when we are called in some way to move forward on our spiritual journey, called to say yes to what is demanded by our healing and growth, called to accept and fulfill God's Will in our lives as it becomes clear to us. And we are called without necessarily feeling that we are up to the challenge, without knowing if or how we could possibly succeed.

Moses can be an interesting and helpful example for us on our journey. He was a such a *human* figure — given to angry outbursts, filled with self-doubts and fears, hindered even by a speech impediment. Nonetheless he heard and responded to God's call to him to help free his brothers and sisters from their suffering. Despite his doubts and fears, he said yes to the call. He moved forward in faith that the strength and power of God would accomplish through him whatever needed to be done.

The Course points out that *"revelation induces complete but temporary suspension of doubt and fear"* (T. p. 4; T-1.II.1:1), and Moses is certainly an example of this. Even after his profound experience of revelation, Moses was far from perfect in his faith. Yet it is also true that each time he doubted, each time he faltered, or became afraid and discouraged, he brought his fears and doubts and concerns to God. Each time he was answered, assured again of God's presence and the certainty of outcome of God's Will. And he would continue on — to falter again and again, yet also growing in faith and stature and authority — toward fulfilling the function God had given him.

Each one of us has a function to fulfill here, given us by God. Jewish mystical tradition teaches that we are *Shutov Elohim*, God's partners, in extending and completing the creation. Stephen Mitchell, in his beautiful work *The Gospel According to Jesus*, offers a fascinating and unusual slant on this idea of what it might mean to help God "complete creation." He renders the famous passage at the beginning of Genesis in this way:

"God completes the work of creation by entering the Sabbath mind, the mind of absolute, joyous serenity; contemplates the whole universe and says, 'Behold, it is very good.'"

> — Stephen Mitchell, *The Gospel According to Jesus*, pp. 12–13

The Course teaches that we each have a "special function" — an indispensable part to play in God's plan for the healing and awakening of His sleeping sons and daughters. It should be stated clearly that, within the framework of the Course, this liberation occurs not through trying to change the conditions of the outer world but through the healing of our own minds. Our task is to attain this state of mind that Mitchell calls "the Sabbath mind." This is the state of mind free of guilt and condemnation, which can look on all through eyes of love and see the reflection of God's presence and love everywhere shining. The particular experiences that make up our life story — our "special function" — provide the unique and individual framework through which we can accomplish that universal goal.

Like Moses we are each called, in our own way, to help release our brothers and sisters, and ourselves with them, from the bondage and oppression of fear, to the freedom and abundance that are our inheritance, and true nature, as children of a loving Father. And like Moses our first response to this call may well be, *"Who am I to be able to do this?"* Yet, also like Moses, we need not be perfect before we can simply open our hearts to hear and say yes to what God asks of us. As the Course teaches, *"readiness... is not mastery"* (M. p. 14; M-4.IX.1:10). We are asked only to offer a little willingness. Our faith and confidence can deepen as we discover, through experience, the truth in God's promise: *"I will be with you."*

True Humility vs. False Humility

"Let us not fight our function. We did not establish it. It is not our idea. The means are given us by which it will be perfectly accomplished. All that we are asked to do is to accept our part in genuine humility, and not deny with self-deceiving arrogance that we are worthy. What is given us to do, we have the strength to do....

"All false humility we lay aside today, that we may listen to God's Voice reveal to us what He would have us do. We do not doubt our adequacy for the function He will offer us. We will be certain only that He knows our strengths, our wisdom and our holiness. And if He deems us worthy, so we are. It is but arrogance that judges otherwise."
            — W. p. 342; W-Pt.I.186.2:1–6; 4

The idea that we are called by God — that not only do we have a part to play in God's plan for healing, but also that our part is essential to the plan's completion — the ego tells us is the epitome of arrogance. The ego's picture of us is that we are small, weak, unworthy, inadequate, filled with darkness. This is the self-image, the self, it would have us accept as our own. Accepting this image of ourselves is what the ego calls humility.

The Course points out, however, that the ego's version of humility is really self-debasement (W. p. 101; W-Pt.I.61.2:1–2) — and is, in fact, disguised arrogance. It is the statement that we are not *God-created* but *self-made* — that our true identity is not the Self that God created but rather what we have made of ourselves. It states that we know ourselves better than God does and therefore know better than He what our function should or should not be.

> *"Your value is in God's Mind. . . . To accept yourself as God created you cannot be arrogance. . . . To accept your littleness is arrogant, because it means that you believe your evaluation of yourself is truer than God's."*
>
> — T. p. 167; T-9.VIII.10:7–9

The function we are called to is, on the deepest level, a single function that we all share. The Course describes this function in many ways — as forgiveness, salvation, healing, accepting the Atonement, offering miracles, reflecting the peace of Heaven here, being the light of the world. These are simply many terms for the same function — allowing love to dispel the fear in us, and light the darkness, allowing the illusion of separation to be undone within our mind, unveiling the truth of Who we are and have always been. We come to know again our oneness in and with God.

"I am the light of the world."

"Who is the light of the world except God's Son? This, then, is merely a statement of the truth about yourself. It is the opposite of a statement of pride, of arrogance, or of self-deception. It does not describe the self concept you have made. . . . It refers to you as you were created by God. It simply states the truth.

"To the ego, today's idea is the epitome of self-glorification. But the ego does not understand humility, mistaking it for self-debasement. Humility consists of accepting your role in salvation and in taking no other. It is not humility to insist you cannot be the light of the world

if that is the function God assigned to you. It is only arrogance that
would assert this function cannot be for you, and arrogance is always
of the ego."

— W. p. 101; W-Pt.I.61.1:1–4, 6–7; 2

False humility, which is really arrogance, attempts to substitute the
ego's concept of what we are for the Self that God created. True humility acknowledges God as our Source and Creator and accepts God's
evaluation of us rather than our own. It recognizes that the strength,
power, wisdom, vision, and whatever else we need to accomplish our
function here comes not from ourselves but is given us by God. It accepts that we can do whatever God asks us to do — because with God
all things are possible — and God is with us at all times and in all
things. To doubt ourselves in what God would have us do is to doubt
God Himself.

"Do as God's Voice directs. And if It asks a thing of you which seems
impossible, remember Who it is That asks, and who would make de-
nial. Then consider this; which is more likely to be right? The Voice
that speaks for the Creator of all things, Who knows all things ex-
actly as they are, or a distorted image of yourself, confused, bewildered,
inconsistent and unsure of everything? Let not its voice direct you.
Hear instead a certain Voice, Which tells you of a function given
you by your Creator Who remembers you, and urges now that you
remember Him."

— W. 344; W-Pt.I.186.12

Accepting Our Function

"Decide that God is right and you are wrong about yourself."
— T. p. 260; T-14.IV.4:5

The Course teaches that we will not be happy unless and until we
fulfill the function God has given us here, that our happiness and our
function are one (W. p. 109; W-Pt.I.66). Happiness comes from being
true to ourselves, true to our deepest selves, our real Self, the Self that
God created. To know this Self we must be willing to drop arrogance
and false humility, to stop insisting that we are less than what God

created us to be. To accept our function, our part in God's plan for salvation and healing, is to side with the truth about ourselves and all of our brothers and sisters.

Our function, the Course tells us, is to *"reflect Heaven here,"* to reflect the peace of Heaven in this world, that the world may be brought to Heaven (T. p. 272; T-14.X.1:6). There are so many times — as we simply go through the normal course of our days, facing countless opportunities for upset and challenges to our inner peace — that this seems to be an impossible task. There are so many times that it appears to us impossible to forgive.

To accept our function means to recognize that on our own fulfilling our function *would* be impossible — but also to recognize that we are not on our own.

Trusting in God's Strength, Not Our Own

"If you are trusting in your own strength, you have every reason to be apprehensive, anxious and fearful. What can you predict or control? What is there in you that can be counted on? What would give you the ability to be aware of all the facets of any problem, and to resolve them in such a way that only good can come of it? What is there in you that gives you the recognition of the right solution, and the guarantee that it will be accomplished?

"Of yourself you can do none of these things. To believe you can is to put your trust where trust is unwarranted. . . .

"It is not by trusting yourself that you will gain confidence. But the strength of God in you is successful in all things."

— W. p. 75; W-Pt.I.47.1, 2:1–2, 5:3–4

Jesus said in the Gospels, *"Of myself I do nothing. It is the Father in me that does the works."* When we accept our function, we acknowledge that God is within us, that there is no separation, and that it is God's strength and wisdom and love within us that accomplish whatever needs to be done. We can move forward, as Moses did, in the faith that we will be able to do what God asks of us because God will be with us. God's Will cannot fail. When we unite our will with His, accepting His as our own, *we* cannot fail.

"...ask yourself if it is possible that God would have a plan for your salvation that does not work. Once you accept His plan as the one function that you would fulfill, there will be nothing else the Holy Spirit will not arrange for you without your effort. He will go before you making straight your path, and leaving in your way no stones to trip on, and no obstacles to bar your way. Nothing you need will be denied you. Not one seeming difficulty but will melt away before you reach it. You need take thought for nothing, careless of everything except the only purpose that you would fulfill. As that was given you, so will its fulfillment be. God's guarantee will hold against all obstacles, for it rests on certainty and not contingency. It rests on **you**. And what can be more certain than a Son of God?"

— T. p. 404; T-20.IV.8:3–12

Chapter 14

Forever in Love

"What would You have me do?
Where would You have me go?
What would you have me say, and to whom?"

— W. p. 121; W-Pt.I.71.9:3–5

"Let us today be neither arrogant nor falsely humble.... We cannot judge ourselves, nor need we do so. These are but attempts to hold decision off, and to delay commitment to our function. It is not our part to judge our worth, nor can we know what role is best for us; what we can do within a larger plan we cannot see in its entirety. Our part is cast in Heaven....

"Whatever your appointed role may be, it was selected by the Voice for God.... Seeing your strengths exactly as they are, and equally aware of where they can be best applied, for what, to whom and when, He chooses and accepts your part for you.

"... that one Voice appoints your function, and relays it to you, giving you the strength to understand it, do what it entails, and to succeed in everything you do that is related to it."

— W. p. 281; W-Pt.I.154.1:1, 3–6,
2:1–2, 3:2

To accept that we have a part to play in God's plan is not arrogance, as the ego would have us believe. Rather it is the beginning of accepting our reality as children of God. It is the willingness to let go of our ego evaluations of ourselves as unworthy, inadequate, weak, and alone in life, and to accept that God's Voice is within us — offering us all the wisdom, strength, energy, courage, direction, and love we need to fulfill what God would have us do. It is true humility, accepting that God's Will is certain and uniting our will with His.

We All Share One Function

In the deepest sense, the part we have in God's plan — our function — is the same for all of us. The Course teaches that our function is *"to accept the Atonement for [ourselves]"* (T. p. 22; T-2.V.5:1), — to allow the belief in separation, with its resulting guilt and fear, to be corrected, undone, in our own minds. As we let our guilt be undone, we remember the Love that we are, the Love that is our real nature, and we reflect that Love to others that they, too, may remember.

The process by which this is accomplished in us is *forgiveness*. Most simply, then, our function is to learn how to forgive, so that we may receive the peace of God that forgiveness brings. We then become examples and teachers of this peace, demonstrating that even in this world peace is possible. We come to reflect the peace of Heaven here on earth.

Although our function is shared, the Course also teaches that we each have a special function in God's plan of healing. In order to understand this teaching and view our own special function in right perspective, we need to look first at the whole idea of "specialness."

Specialness — The Ego's "Gift"

The world of the ego — this world of form — is a world of *differences*. Although the Course teaches that our reality is oneness, in this world there are certainly differences among us. We have different talents, abilities, strengths, backgrounds, and life experiences. The ego uses these differences to separate out, to divide and make "specialness" categories of superiority and inferiority, insiders and outsiders, "haves" and "have-nots." Specialness is grounded in comparisons. The ego, the Course tells us, *"literally lives by comparisons"* (T. p. 52; T-4.II.7:1).

In this world we normally accept without question that being special is a good thing. We value and even cherish specialness. Yet this sense of specialness, which, being so ego-identified, we all seek, always serves to separate us, to set us apart from others in some way. As the Course points out, specialness inevitably reinforces our belief in separation — and thus inevitably reinforces our conscious and unconscious guilt and fear as well.

If we see ourselves as better than another by virtue of a particular talent or ability we have, in our minds we have attacked their intrinsic wholeness and value. We will — consciously or not — feel or see ourselves as guilty. If we are envious of someone else's talents or life experiences or feel that we are lacking because we don't have something that they have, we attack our own wholeness. On some level in our minds we will resent and blame them for our feelings of inferiority and lack. Again, we will feel guilty.

According to the Course, specialness — particularly the idea of "special love" — is the ego's most cherished and boasted "gift" to us (T. p. 317; T-16.V.3:1). It is also the most insidious, because we rarely look at it closely enough to question its worth, value, and cost to us. The real cost is enormous, because, the Course points out, the ego offers us specialness in place of — as a substitute for — the Love of God.

God's Love is not special. God's Love for any of us cannot be special, because God's Love is complete and whole. God loves all His children equally, because He loves us all totally. His total Love gives us everything. The idea of specialness is the insane belief that we could want and have more than everything.

The Course teaches that the Holy Spirit is God's Answer to the ego, to the belief in separation. The Holy Spirit's function is to translate all that the ego made for its purpose — of reinforcing separation, guilt, and fear — into what can serve the purpose of wholeness and healing — the undoing of separation, guilt, and fear. Although the ego made the idea of specialness for its unholy purpose, the Holy Spirit translates it into the idea of our special function — the unique part we each play in God's plan for healing us all.

Our Special Function

*"Each has a special part to play in the Atonement, but the message
given to each one is always the same; **God's Son is guiltless.** Each one
teaches the message differently, and learns it differently. Yet until he
teaches and learns it, he will suffer the dim awareness that his true
function remains unfulfilled in him."*

— T. p. 262; T-14.V.2:1–3

Our shared true function is to teach and learn the healing lesson
of guiltlessness, through the practice of forgiveness. What the Course
calls our special function essentially refers to the specific, particular relationships, situations, and ways in which we can teach and learn this
single lesson.

We are all teachers and learners all the time. The Holy Spirit's purpose for every relationship and every encounter we have with anyone
is to have it be a *"holy relationship"* — to help us transcend our differences, recognize and forgive our projections of guilt, and remember
the Love of God that is within us both and joins us together as one.

Although, the Course points out, there is no one from whom we
cannot learn, and thus no one we cannot teach, from a practical standpoint we cannot meet everyone. The plan of the Atonement therefore
includes specific contacts to be made in each of our lives (M. p. 6;
M-3.1) Some of these will be direct, personal, ongoing relationships.
Others will appear to be superficial, casual, momentary encounters in
which we never learn each other's names.

There are even situations in which we never "meet" at all. We may
read a newspaper story about someone, or listen to a musician perform,
or hear about a person going through an illness, or notice someone's
kindness to a stranger, or read a book someone has written, and be
touched or triggered by that "encounter" in a way that furthers our
healing, growth, and learning.

The Course teaches that none of this is accidental, that *"there are
no accidents in salvation"* (M. p. 6; M-3.1:6). There are those we are
meant to encounter, directly or indirectly, and these will inevitably
cross our life path, our awareness, in some way. To use these specific
relationships and encounters as opportunities for forgiveness and heal-

ing, as places we can learn and teach the love that we are, is our special function.

Our Special Function and Abilities

This special function, our unique part in God's plan, may be expressed through — but is not defined by or limited to — our profession or our particular talents and abilities. The work we do in the world is one of the ways we may be brought together with the people we are meant to meet, one of the settings in which we can teach and learn. The specific talents and abilities we have may help to determine some of the forms through which we can best communicate and receive the Holy Spirit's message of peace.

The Course teaches that differences in talents and abilities among God's children are temporary — part of the temporal world of the ego, not of the reality of Heaven.

"When the Atonement has been completed, all talents will be shared by all the Sons of God. God is not partial. All His children have His total Love, and all His gifts are freely given to everyone alike."
— T. p. 10; T-1.V.3:1–3

While we still believe in the reality of the ego and the world of form, however, differences in abilities and talents are a fact of our experience. What we need to decide is which master we would have them serve — the ego or God.

The ego will use these differences for self-serving purposes, for its own inflation, to shatter the unity of God's creation by seemingly establishing hierarchies of value or worth. Smarter, stronger, funnier, more attractive, musical, athletic, verbal, charming, artistic, spiritual, psychic, or whatever — all become, in the ego's eyes, "better": more worthy, more lovable, more loved. Some are included in the "specialness club," while others are excluded.

Even among spiritual seekers, a belief in "special abilities" that result in or represent a "special connection" with God or the higher realms is often found. Holding such a belief, whether in regard to ourselves or others, can serve only to delay our awakening.

Given over to the Holy Spirit, our abilities and talents will be utilized to serve the undoing of our experience of difference and separation, from each other and from God. They will be used to help us learn that whatever differences exist among us at the level of form make no difference whatsoever in God's eyes — in our inherent value and worth as an integral part of God's creation. We are all "included."

When we offer ourselves — all that we believe that we are — to the Holy Spirit to be retranslated and used only for His purpose and plan, our lives here become a living expression of love and service. The longing for this full surrender to and joining with love is the deepest yearning of our hearts.

FOREVER IN LOVE

I'll go where You would have me go,
I'll do what You would have me do,
I'll be forever in Love with You, my God

I'll touch who You would have me touch
I'll see what You would have me see
I'll be forever in Love with You

I'll give what You would have me give
I'll feed who You would have me feed
I'll be forever in Love with You, my God

I'll play what You would have me play
I'll sing what You would have me sing
I'll be forever in Love with You

And I'll dance in the light of Your Love
Forever in Love with You, my God
I'll dance in the light of Your Love
Forever in Love with You
Only You . . .

— Donna Cary, "Forever in Love"
from *Real Love*

Our Essential Part

The wholeness of Creation is incomplete without any of us. We are all part of it, and we are all equally indispensable.

"You are altogether irreplaceable in the Mind of God. No one else can fill your part in it, and while you leave your part empty your eternal place merely waits for your return. God, through His Voice, reminds you of it."

— T. p. 167; T-9.VIII.10:1

Accepting our part in God's plan is remembering that we have an eternal place in the unity of creation and recognizing that we need to help each other remember and awaken to that reality. Our special function is to help those who cross our life path, for they have been, in a sense, entrusted to us by God. And we help them by being willing to see the face of Christ in them — by recognizing and forgiving the projections and illusions we have looked upon instead. As we offer them release, we are set free with them.

We need not know the whole plan nor even how to fulfill our part in it. If we are willing, we can trust that we will be shown and guided.

"I will accept my part in God's plan for salvation."

"... Give Him the words, and He will do the rest. He will enable you to understand your special function. He will open up the way to happiness, and peace and trust will be His gifts; His answer to your words.... And you will have conviction then of Him Who knows the function you have on earth as well as Heaven."

— W. p. 173; W-Pt.I.98.9:1–3, 5

Just as Moses was assured when he answered God's call to him to lead his brothers and sisters to freedom, we too are assured of success in our function — because God will be with us. Any doubts we have along the way are simply attempts by the ego to keep us forgetful of who we really are, and Who makes sure our way. Yet we will fulfill our function, for God's Will for us is fulfillment.

"If you knew Who walks beside you
on the way that you have chosen,
fear would be impossible."

— T. p. 353; T-18.III.3:2

"Your feet are safely set upon the road that leads the world to God.
... Forget not He has placed His Hand in yours, and given you your
brothers in His Trust that you are worthy of His Trust in you. ... His
Trust has made your pathway certain and your goal secure. You will
not fail your brothers nor your Self."

— W. p. 286; W-Pt.I.155.13:1, 4, 6–7

The Outcome Is Certain and
Guaranteed by God

" 'Who walks with me?' This question should be asked a thousand
times a day, till certainty has ended doubting and established peace.
Today let doubting cease. ... "

— W. p. 288; W-Pt.I.156.8:1–3

We can rest in the assurance that we can do what God would have
us do. We will awaken to the freedom and awareness of perfect oneness that is Heaven, and all our brothers and sisters with us. We will
say yes to God's call in us, for it is our own deepest longing as well.
And the outcome is as certain as God.

"Forget not once this journey is begun the end is certain. Doubt along
the way will come and go and go to come again. Yet is the ending
sure. No one can fail to do what God appointed him to do. When you
forget, remember that you walk with Him and with His Word upon
your heart. Who could despair when Hope like this is his? Illusions of
despair may seem to come, but learn how not to be deceived by them.
Behind each one there is reality and there is God. ... The end is sure
and guaranteed by God."

— M. p. 87; C-Epilogue.1:1–8, 10

Like Moses, we can accept our part in God's plan. Like Moses,
we need not be perfect. We need but bring the doubts and fears that

threaten our peace, again and again, to the Holy Spirit, and we will hear in some way the same answer Moses heard — the single Answer God has given us all.

> *"I will be with you —*
> *as I have been with you always —*
> *as I am with you now."*

Chapter 15

"Love Always Answers": A Personal Account

Part 1 — An Experience of Forgiveness

"And what you call with love will come to you. Love always answers, being unable to deny a call for help, or to hear the cries of pain that rise to it from every part of this strange world you made but do not want. All that you need to give this world away in glad exchange for what you did not make is willingness to learn the one you made is false."

— T. p. 237; T-13.VII.4:2–4

Even on the spiritual path, working purposely day to day to be aware and present, life sometimes becomes routine. We get caught up in our work, our responsibilities, our relationships. We address and deal with those problems and issues and healing opportunities that present themselves, and life proceeds more or less "on course."

And then one day life includes or presents something unexpected — perhaps dramatic — and suddenly everything changes. We are flung into a heightened awareness, confronted with a healing and learning possibility of greater than ordinary magnitude and challenge.

We may be forced to look further and deeper into ourselves, into what we believe and what we value. We may be forced to reevaluate how we have been going about our lives, how we have been making decisions and choices. We may be lifted to a new level of understanding or carried to a deeper level of our practice. We may be accelerated on our spiritual healing journey, brought into closer or more immediate experience of Spirit's presence with and within us. Certainly we emerge from the experience different than we entered.

A few years ago my life included such an experience — a sudden and serious illness that required a ten-day hospitalization. It proved to be a time rich in learning, healing, insight, and opportunity to practice my path.

> *"This is not a course in the play of ideas*
> *but in their practical application."*
>
> — T. p. 196; T-11.VIII.5.3

Entering the hospital propelled me into what felt like a greatly expanded challenge and opportunity to "practice what I preach" — to be very conscious of and purposeful in applying the ideas and principles of the Course to the situations confronting me.

What I relearned and came to appreciate most powerfully through this experience — and in so many different ways — is the *centrality of relationship* in our healing process. The Course's teaching that sickness is separation and that healing is joining became very apparent and very real to me.

I also came through this experience with a deeper knowing and certainty that there are no accidental relationships or encounters in our lives, that every relationship, every encounter we have with anyone is part of the overall plan for our healing. Every relationship, every encounter, every moment within our own thoughts, offers us an opportunity to choose between separation and joining, between judgment and acceptance, between fear and love. And although I continue, in my own process, to forget again and again, I learned that in truth there is really only once choice we *want* to make.

> *"It's all about love — tell everybody."*
> — Jeff Buzzetti, AIDS Quilt

The Ego's Battleground — "Us vs. Them"

"The Holy Spirit's temple is not a body, but a relationship."
— T. p. 407; T-20.VI.5:1

I was admitted to the hospital on the day of the verdict in the first Rodney King trial and of the start of the rioting in Los Angeles. As that city exploded in an extreme and dramatic depiction of the consequences of "us vs. them" thinking, I quickly had the chance to witness exactly the same ego thought system in my own mind with respect to the hospital staff and patients.

By the time I was admitted, I was physically exhausted and drained. What I had mistakenly thought was a back problem combined with the flu was in fact a deep kidney infection. My right kidney had abscessed, and the poisons from the infection had spilled into my blood stream. For nearly a week I had had a 101-degree fever, been in continuous physical pain, and eaten nothing but a little soup each day.

I had not been a patient in a hospital since I was twelve years old, and then only overnight for a knee injury. Entering the hospital was a little like traveling to a foreign culture. Everything was unfamiliar. I didn't know what was happening or what to expect. I felt like a stranger in a *very* strange land.

From the start, the hospital staff, particularly the nurses and aides, seemed very busy and unresponsive. When I got to my room — after what felt like countless intake interviews with different people asking the same questions and a few hours worth of routine and emergency tests — I found that there was no call button hooked up by the bed, no way to call the staff. I felt vulnerable, isolated, and stranded.

It took several requests over a period of time to get this corrected. Eventually one of the resident doctors on call that night hooked up a makeshift system that worked. Over the next few days I discovered that at least two other beds in my room had the same problem. The patients in those beds were bedridden. They could call for nursing staff help only by hollering and hoping eventually to be heard.

During the first few days I witnessed a number of incidents of what appeared to be harsh, impatient, insensitive treatment of patients by the staff — some seeming almost to verge on cruelty. The staff, who were there to help, seemed more like the enemy.

As I started to feel a little better physically, I began to recognize that my perception of the nursing staff — the "us against them" war that was raging within my own thoughts — was greatly in need of healing. I saw that the perception I had was very conducive to frustration, fear, and upset — and not at all conducive to inner peace. I became aware that it was this perception, and not any physical pain I was still having, that was the real source of the suffering I was feeling at times.

Opening to Healing

At the time, all I knew was that I needed a different perception, another way to look at and see the nursing staff. I also recognized that I couldn't come up with one on my own. I had a conversation in my mind with the Holy Spirit, describing my experience and perception and asking for help to see differently.

I soon had the simple thought, "These people are also human beings. Reach out to them." I found myself starting to express interest in the staff when they would come in to change my I.V. bag or take my blood pressure, commenting on how busy and demanding their jobs seemed to be, asking how their day was going or how they were this evening, and so on. And I found that I was genuinely interested, not simply making conversation. These really were human beings, just like me — and they responded with warmth and appreciation to my simple interest in and concern for them.

Over the rest of my time in the hospital, tremendous healing took place within my own mind, a complete undoing of the "us against them" ego thinking that I had started with. As this occurred I was able to extend love, and I had some very moving experiences with several of the nurses.

I discovered that what had appeared to me as insensitivity and lack of caring was in fact the expression of frustration. These were, for the most part, genuinely caring and competent people who were overworked because the hospital was understaffed. They felt unappreciated and demoralized by a system that didn't allow them enough time and energy, after handling all the technical demands and documentation requirements of their jobs, to devote to the caregiving aspect of nursing that had attracted them to the profession in the first place.

Those I talked to were so appreciative of being able to express their feelings, so appreciative of having someone listen with a sympathetic ear and understand. One nurse, Virginia, shared with me her "secret" aspiration to someday develop a volunteer program to meet some of the simple caregiving and companionship needs that so often now go unmet in hospitals. She hugged me as she went off shift the day I was to be discharged and said she would never forget me. I know that I will not forget her either.

Another, Carolyn, began to cry when I told her how much her cheerful personality and energy brightened the whole atmosphere on the floor and how much I appreciated her presence. She remarked that no one ever said things like that to the nurses and that my feedback had "made" her whole day.

Yvette had her first "solo" shift during my stay, after two consecutive nights of being trained by and working with a supervisor. She had seemed overwhelmed and unsure of herself during the training nights, but did fine her first night on her own. I congratulated her at the end of her shift, wanting to acknowledge and support her sense of accomplishment. She seemed very grateful to have someone recognize and share in this milestone in her career.

In a tape series from his workshop "The Unhealed Healer," Ken Wapnick points out that our ostensible role, or seeming purpose, in a given situation is not necessarily our real or deepest healing purpose in that setting. Although I was, at the level of form, the "patient" in this situation, I was also there — on a deeper level — to *offer* healing as well.

The Practice of Forgiveness

"When you meet anyone, remember it is a holy encounter. As you see him you will see yourself. As you treat him you will treat yourself. As you think of him you will think of yourself. Never forget this, for in him you will find yourself or lose yourself.... Give him his place in the Kingdom and you will have yours."

— T. p. 132; T-8.III.4:1–5, 5:12

Although I had not been thinking specifically in terms of practicing forgiveness when I asked for help in changing my perception of the nursing staff, in retrospect the steps of the forgiveness process are clear.

As we looked at in chapter 3, Ken Wapnick has summarized the forgiveness process — the basic spiritual practice of the Course — as involving three steps (Kenneth Wapnick, *A Talk Given on A Course in Miracles*, 3rd edition, pp. 69–73).

The first step is recognizing and accepting that the problem is not "out there" — in someone else or what someone else is doing — but rather that the problem is within us, in the guilt within our own minds. The Course asks us to work with a premise that if we are upset and bothered by something in someone else, it is because they are showing us a *mirror* of something we would rather not see in ourselves.

I was perceiving the nursing staff initially as uncaring and insensitive to our (the patients') needs. They did not appear to me to have much compassion for us as people in pain and instead seemed to react frequently out of impatience and irritation.

The Course points out that if we are focusing on and reacting to another's ego, we must be seeing through our own (T. p. 155; T-9.III.3, 4). I was clearly viewing the nursing staff through my own egocentric viewpoint. From the perspective of my ego, the fact is that I was concerned only about my own needs. I wanted the nurses to respond right away when I needed something. At those moments, I certainly had no compassion for what is involved in attending to the care of a sizable number of people. I gave no thought to where else they might be or who else they might be attending to. When they didn't drop everything to respond to my need, I reacted (at least within my own mind) with impatience and irritation. Everything I was seeing in them was, in fact, a reflection of the stance and position of my own ego. This is not a statement of self-blame, but merely an observation and description of the state of mind I was in at the time.

The second step of the forgiveness process is to recognize that the real problem, the source of our pain, is not *what we see*, but rather our *judgment and condemnation* of what we see. The real problem is that we see the manifestations of ego (in the other and in ourselves) as sins, symbols of guilt and deserving of punishment.

Within my own mind I was judging these expressions of ego —

insensitivity to and lack of concern for the needs or experience of others — as something terrible, something to feel guilty about, something that warranted condemnation and attack. While overtly I was judging the nurses, covertly I was also condemning myself — and this was the deeper source of my upset and fear.

In the second step of the forgiveness process, then, we recognize that we need another way to see — a different perception that releases and undoes our judgment of guilt.

The third step in the forgiveness process involves

1. the willingness to recognize that there is an Alternative within us — another perspective, another perception that is not that of the ego, and

2. the willingness to join with, to see from, that other perspective.

The third step is asking the Holy Spirit — the Presence of Love within our minds — to help us change our minds, to help us see differently, and allowing a new perception to be given us. We do not "figure it out." Rather, it occurs to us as an idea or thought that leads us back to inner peace. For me the thought, "These people are also human beings; reach out to them," was Love's answer to my call for help.

As we are willing to rejoin with God's Love within us — undoing our inner experience of separation — the outer expressions of separation in our relationships may also begin to dissolve. Separation and fear are replaced by understanding, connectedness, and the love that is our natural state of relationship with one another.

My experience with the nursing staff provided me with a vivid and powerful experience of this process of healing through forgiveness, for which I am deeply grateful.

Chapter 16

"Love Always Answers":
A Personal Account

Part 2 — Choosing a Holy Purpose

Times of crisis or difficulty often have a way of bringing us into closer or deeper communication with God, as we turn to Him for strength, comfort, direction, and right perspective. My hospital stay was such a time for me.

Ostensibly I was in the hospital to receive medical treatment for a physical illness — and this certainly was one form in which I could experience healing, through joining in purpose with the doctors and nurses who were treating and caring for me. Yet what was also very clear to me, nearly from the outset of the experience, was the potential this situation in my life offered me for a much deeper level of healing and growth.

This deeper level of healing — which the Course calls true healing and not simply "magic" — is a healing of *mind*. It is the undoing of another layer of the belief in separation, guilt, and fear that lies at the core of our identification with the ego. Such healing is a turning back to, a reuniting with the Love of God already present in our hearts and minds. As we learn that we are not, in truth, separated from God's Love — and never have been — we discover too that we are not separate from other people, but rather are joined with them by and in this Love.

The Course teaches that healing is the result of changing our minds — of the willingness to have our perceptions and thoughts be

143

corrected — of the decision to choose love and joining over fear and separation. This change of mind and perception is what the Course refers to as a *miracle*. Although the miracle is an internal shift, the Course also teaches that

> *"Miracles.... are genuinely interpersonal, and result in true closeness to others. Revelation unites you directly with God. Miracles unite you directly with your brother."*
>
> — T. p. 5; T-1.II.1:4–6

The experience of healing teaches us that minds are truly joined, that we are separate neither from God nor from each other. A deepened experience and expanded awareness of our interconnectedness, of the shared nature of healing, was pervasive during my time in the hospital — and was an important and powerful aspect of the healing, learning, and growth offered to me by this experience.

Choosing a Holy Purpose

Early in my hospital stay, I became vividly aware that — beneath the outer form and purpose, beyond the role of being a patient in a hospital — there could be a holy purpose for the situation in which I found myself, the purpose of opening to true healing in myself and offering healing to others — if I were willing to choose that purpose for the experience.

> *"This is the lesson God would have you learn:*
> *There is a way to look on everything*
> *that lets it be to you another step to Him...."*
>
> — W. p. 359; W-Pt.I.193.13:1

The awareness of this possibility, and the choice to have the situation serve a deeper purpose and meaning, was a central focus of my time in the hospital. It was the source of a profound sense of God's presence, and often filled me with a joyful and overflowing sense of gratitude. At times I lay in bed and wept for how blessed I felt by the whole experience. It literally felt like a gift of love from God.

I was especially grateful for the deepening in my inner knowing of a truth I had already recognized — that "doing our work," fulfilling our part in God's plan, is *not* a matter of outer form. It is not limited to an occupation, or to a particular time, place, or setting. It does not require any particular type of relationship, or being in any particular social roles.

Everywhere we are, every moment of our lives, every situation in which we find ourselves offers us the opportunity to do our real work here — to accept healing for ourselves and to offer healing to our sisters and brothers.

Our "Special Function"

"When I am healed, I am not healed alone."
— W. p. 254; W-Pt.I.137

"Those who are healed become instruments of healing."
— W. p. 255; W-Pt.I.137.11:1

As we open to receive healing, we automatically offer healing to others. The light of the Holy Spirit in our minds reaches out to join with that same light in the minds of all who are in any way connected with us through this experience.

"The power of one mind can shine into another, because all the lamps of God were lit by the same spark. It is everywhere and It is eternal."
— T. p. 175; T-10.IV.7:5–6

In this joining, we both teach and learn the lesson that separation is illusory. As we offer to others the reminder of God's ever-present love for and within us, we are strengthened in our own remembering as well.

The Course teaches that we each have a special function here, a part that is uniquely ours in the overall plan of the Atonement. Our special function refers in part to the specific people and relationships that are part of our life experience.

The Course states clearly that there are no accidental encounters in our lives. Everyone we interact with in any way — no matter how briefly, no matter how seemingly casual or "impersonal" the encounter — is part of our teaching-learning assignment in the eyes of the Holy Spirit. The Holy Spirit's purpose for every one of these relationships is healing — the learning of forgiveness, the undoing of separation and of the belief that we are alone, the extending of love.

I found it tremendously helpful to view my hospitalization in light of the idea of my special function. There were so many people I interacted with simply by virtue of being in the hospital — nurses, aides, doctors, medical students, other patients. There were friends I spent more time with, on the phone or during their visits, than I might have had I been involved in my normal life schedule and activities. Several experiences I had early in my hospital stay helped me to be conscious that every interaction I had with anyone there held the potential for receiving and/or offering healing.

The Gift of Kindness

My first night in the hospital was extremely arduous and difficult. I was exhausted, frightened, nearly dehydrated, and in tremendous physical pain. At one point, after being taken for a sonogram and then brought back to my room, my fever spiked to 103 degrees, and my body went into near convulsions. A little while later one of the medical residents told me I was going to be taken down for X-rays and then would possibly have some kind of treatment procedure done that night as well.

I felt as though I had reached my limits of endurance, that I couldn't possibly handle any more exertion, strain, or pain, that something inside me was going to break. But the doctors needed the tests to have a clearer idea of what was going on, and medically I needed the treatment procedure — so it seemed I had no choice. I felt trapped in a nightmare. I prayed for help, asking to feel the presence and comfort of the Holy Spirit with me.

My prayer was quickly answered in the form of the hospital escort who took me down to X-ray. He was an elderly gentleman, whose quiet, easy manner reminded me of the Morgan Freeman character in the film "Driving Miss Daisy." He was very gentle, polite, pleasant, and kind. He had been doing this same job for nearly thirty years, he said, and was glad to have work that involved helping people. I felt very calmed and reassured simply by his presence and kindness. I never learned his name, but I will always remember him and the gift of healing he offered me that night.

While the outer circumstances were still the same, the inner quality of my experience had dramatically shifted. I had been released from my nightmare of isolation and fear. I felt myself in the presence of love, expressed through simple human kindness.

As it happened, the outer situation also began to ease. After the X-rays it was decided that my condition was stable enough to wait till the next day to do the treatment procedure. The intense physical strain and ordeal was over for the night as well.

For me that night, one person's simple choice to be helpful and kind had carried within it all the healing power of God's Love. It was a clear and dramatic lesson as well as a gift.

Our Choice to Make,
Our Gift to Give

A few mornings later, I awoke to the sound of the woman in the next bed moaning in pain. I was suddenly filled with an acute awareness of the enormity of suffering in the world. I thought, "There are four of us in this room alone and how many rooms are there on this floor, how many floors in the hospital, how many hospitals in this city... how many people are ill and suffering in their homes, as I was last week... how many millions of people all over the world, suffering — not only physical pain, but so many other forms of suffering and pain as well...."

I felt overwhelmed and helpless. I didn't know what to do with this awareness, with the sense of human connection I felt with all those people and the longing to help. The perspective that this reality is a dream offered little comfort. Within the dream, suffering is subjectively very real to those experiencing it.

I prayed for help, spontaneously directing my asking to Jesus, Mary, and Buddha — for me all symbols of profound compassion, love, and wisdom. I asked, "How can I keep my heart open in the face of all the suffering felt in the world? I know you must see differently than I am seeing. Please help me to see as you see."

I did not receive a verbal answer of any kind. Yet as the morning went on, I found that I was very aware of having a choice to make, in each moment and each interaction I had. In every encounter, I was faced with the choice either to reach beyond myself (whether in action or simply in thought) in kindness and love, or to separate myself through judgment, withdrawal, apathy, or fear.

In this awareness I recognized my answer. I could use each moment — with whoever was right in front of me, either physically or in my thoughts — to choose kindness instead of harshness, understanding instead of judgment, acceptance instead of attack. In every moment I was either deepening and increasing the experience of suffering in the world, or helping in some small way to alleviate it — through my simple choice.

I saw that each choice I made for kindness and love, no matter how seemingly small, carried with it the same full healing power of God's love that I had received through another's kindness a few nights before. I understood in a deeper way the teaching in the Course that *"all expressions of love are maximal"* (T. p. 1; T-1.I.1:3).

Saying Yes to My Function

These experiences helped me to be very clear about the purpose of my being in the hospital: I was there to learn to experience more fully God's love for me and to be a messenger of that love to those around me, to those affected in any way by my being there.

Almost from the beginning, I had little or no concern or question about my eventual physical recovery. I had a real sense of joining and common purpose with my doctor, a firm conviction that God's healing can be expressed as easily through the form of conventional medical treatment as any other way, and a strong sense that this experience was preparing me for another level of sharing, teaching, and learning.

Given that I am still very ego-identified, I am certain that my inner assurance of physical recovery made it easier for me to focus on the deeper healing opportunities the Holy Spirit was making so abundantly available each day. I have a deep respect and gratitude for those who manage to live and demonstrate this focus on opening to and extending love *without* the certainty or likelihood of physical recovery. What a light and example they offer to me, to us all.

Chapter 17

"Love Always Answers":
A Personal Account

Part 3 — Exchanging the Nightmare
for the Happy Dream

Accepting Healing

The awareness of a deeper level of meaning and purpose to the experience was an anchor for me during my illness and hospital stay and was often the source of a profound sense of God's presence with me, of His hand at work in the situation, and of His greater plan for the healing of all His separated sons and daughters.

The Course teaches that our only function here is to accept the Atonement — the undoing of our belief that we are separate from God and from each other — for ourselves (T. p. 22; T-2.V.5:1). The result of accepting the Atonement — accomplished through the miracle, or the changing of our perceptions and thoughts — is the experience of healing. Because minds are joined, as we accept healing for ourselves, we automatically extend healing to others.

The Holy Spirit, God's Answer to the separation, is already and forever present within our minds, reminding us always of God's abiding love and care for us. We do not hear this reminder only because we have distracted ourselves and filled our minds instead with thoughts of separation — thoughts of sickness, guilt, victimization, deprivation, blame, unworthiness, and fear. When we have finally had enough of the pain generated by these thoughts, we can choose to let them be replaced by the gentle reassurance and message of the Voice for God.

> *"The Holy Spirit's Voice is as loud*
> *as your willingness to listen."*
>
> — T. p. 145; T-8.VIII.8:7

Accepting healing is simply accepting the truth that we are *already healed* — for if the Holy Spirit is already with and within our minds, then we cannot be separate from the Mind of God, Who is perfect Life and Wholeness and Peace. Yet within our experience here, in the world of form and time, the healing "journey" we travel is the process of becoming more and more aware of the Holy Spirit's presence in us — of turning more and more of our thinking, perceiving, and decision-making over to His direction and guidance.

The Course teaches that we become increasingly aware of the Holy Spirit in us by His effects (T. p. 161; T-9.VI.1:1). We can see His effect on others as we offer forgiveness and love. And we can experience the inner peace that comes to us — usually in ways we could not have imagined, designed, or thought up on our own — when we ask for help to see differently and are willing to let the causes of the fear in our minds be illuminated and undone.

Asking for Help —
What Do I Want to See/Experience?

As I shared in the last chapter, my first night in the hospital began as a real nightmare. I felt stressed to my limit, physically, emotionally, mentally. I was in considerable pain and felt very frightened and alone.

As I was about to be taken for X-rays, I remembered a metaphor Ken Wapnick offered in a workshop I had taken on "Time: The Vast Illusion." He had suggested that we can think of our experience here as like watching a videotape that we have selected to view. But we have gotten so caught up in the story on the screen that we seem to have "lost" ourselves. We have projected ourselves into the action. We've forgotten that who we are is the one who selected and is watching the tape — and not the central character of the story on the screen.

In this analogy, for every tape in our "video library," there are two different versions of it — the ego's version and the Holy Spirit's version. Regardless of the particular plot line, every one of the ego's tapes has the same underlying content — separation, guilt, fear, loss, and pain. For each one of these, the Holy Spirit has a corresponding tape, with an entirely different content. The content of the Holy Spirit's tapes is always healing, forgiveness, love, joy — the undoing of separation and all its seeming effects. Our decision, our only real decision, is which of these two versions we want to see and experience at any given moment in time.

Practically, this means recognizing when we have chosen to watch the ego's version of a given "tape" —

1. noticing that we seem to be in the midst of a horror movie

2. accepting that we have, on some level, *chosen* to experience that, and

3. deciding that we don't like the tape we are watching and would rather see the Holy Spirit's version instead.

It is not our responsibility to try to write or make up what we think the Holy Spirit's tape would be. It is our responsibility only to recognize that we are the maker of the experience we don't like (by our choice to watch the ego's tape), and therefore that it is possible for us to change our minds and experience the Holy Spirit's tape in place of the ego's.

This analogy essentially restates the process described in chapter 28 of the Text of the Course, in the section entitled "Reversing Effect and Cause." Here we are asked to recognize that we are the dreamer and not the hero of our dream of separation, guilt, and fear. Regardless of how it may seem, we are not helpless victims of a world of other people and circumstances that seem to be outside of us. Rather, our experience reflects back to us what we have chosen in our minds to see and experience as real.

Recognizing the power of the choice in our minds to determine our experience also empowers us to choose differently if we decide we don't like and don't want the experience we are having. It is this recognition that the responsibility for our experience rests within our minds, in our inner choice — rather than in anything that seems to be outside us — that is the *miracle,* and that opens the way for our healing.

> *"The miracle does not awaken you, but merely shows you who the dreamer is. It teaches you there is a choice of dreams while you are still asleep, depending on the purpose of your dreaming. Do you wish for dreams of healing, or dreams of death? A dream is like a memory in that it pictures what you wanted shown to you.*
> *"... if you are the dreamer, you perceive this much at least: That you have caused the dream, and can accept another dream as well. But for this change in content of the dream, it must be realized that it is you who dreamed the dreaming that you do not like. It is but an effect that you have caused, and you would not be cause of this effect."*
> — T. p. 551; T-28.II.4:2–4, 5:2–4

Again, our responsibility in a practical sense is simply to be willing to say, "The experience I'm having right now feels like a nightmare. On some level I must have made the choice to experience this, because this is what I'm experiencing. I want to make a different choice, because I don't like how this feels — I don't want this."

Not wanting the nightmare, we want a real alternative — the Holy Spirit's version of the videotape, or what the Course calls the *"happy dream."* We do not, on our own, supply this alternative. We merely ask for it — offering the willingness to have it be given to us — recognizing that it is this we really want — and letting go of any investment in the version we have made.

> *"... in forgiving dreams is no one asked to be the victim and the sufferer. These are the happy dreams the miracle exchanges for your own. It does not ask that you make another; only that you see you made the one you would exchange for this."*
> — T. p. 551; T-28.II.5:6–8

> *"... what you leave as vacant God will fill...."*
> — T. p. 532; T-27.III.4:3

That first night in the hospital, I very much needed to make use of this perspective. My prayer took the form of acknowledging that I was experiencing myself in a nightmare — that from where I was looking I couldn't imagine how the situation could look or feel or be any different — but that I was open to the possibility that there was an alternative, the Holy Spirit's version, and that I would rather experience that instead.

Receiving God's Answer

The Course teaches that it is the Holy Spirit's task, assigned to Him by God, to supply the alternative to our nightmare — and that He will always respond to our sincere asking, to the simple openness and desire of our hearts. His alternative may or may not involve a change in the outer circumstances of our situation — but it will always result in a change in our inner experience of the situation. Fear and suffering will dissolve and be replaced by an experience of safety and peace.

"God's answer is some form of peace."
— W. p. 474; W-Pt.II.359

As I have shared, the transformation of my experience that night began through the kindness of the man who was assigned to escort me to X-ray. I felt calmed and reassured by his gentle manner and presence and knew on some level that this was an answer to my prayer.

The transformation continued in the course of my having the X-rays taken. The technician was a pleasant and friendly young man. Much to my surprise — given how thoroughly exhausted and overwhelmed I had been feeling only minutes before — I heard myself initiate "small talk" with him. We chatted about his wife and child and their plans for his upcoming weekend off. I shared that I had done my psychology internship in that same hospital fifteen years before and that it was very different to be there in the role of patient.

I say that I was surprised because I literally did not know where inside of me that conversation came from. It certainly did not come from my ego, as I had not been feeling at all friendly or sociable. Yet it did come from *something* within me — and I recognized that it was fostering an experience of healing and relief.

As we chatted, I felt myself becoming more relaxed and at ease. At one point, one of the X-rays needed to be retaken; he had set the machine too high or low. I was still in great physical pain and was very much wanting to get back to my room and sleep. Yet instead of being upset by this delay, I found myself thinking, "So, he made a mistake — it's no big deal." When I needed something to prop up my knees to ease the pain in my back, he readily went and found some extra blankets to use for that purpose.

The young resident who, a short time before, had seemed very much the "enemy" in my sight for telling me that I needed to have more tests and procedures done that night, also came into the X-ray room. I learned that he had stayed an hour over his shift to make sure I was all right and to let me know that the treatment procedure could wait till the next day. I experienced a genuine caring from him and felt very moved by and grateful for his concern.

Whereas I had been feeling very alone, isolated, and alien, I now felt among friends. My spirits had definitely been lifted and even my physical discomfort seemed to diminish. It was apparent to me that I could not, on my own, have engineered such a dramatic change in my experience. Nor could I have predicted how it would occur. But I didn't have to. I needed only to do my small part. The Holy Spirit gladly did His.

I found it necessary to use this perspective a number of times during my hospital stay. I would find myself feeling helpless and frustrated by circumstances beyond my control — recognize that my experience of the situation as a nightmare was of my own choosing, and not the only possibility — and ask to experience the Holy Spirit's version instead of my own. Each time Love answered in a way I could not have predicted or orchestrated.

Through these experiences I was given the enormous gift — in return for my simple asking — of a greater awareness and deepening trust in His presence and help in my mind and in my life. As this occurred, I also became more and more aware of the opportunities and ways He could, and wanted to, extend through me to bless and heal others as well.

Chapter 18

"Love Always Answers":
A Personal Account

Part 4—The Shared Nature of Healing

"When I am healed, I am not healed alone.
And I would bless my brothers,
for I would be healed with them,
as they are healed with me."

—W. p. 256; W-Pt.I.137.15:5–6

A deeper realization and experience of the interconnectedness we share, humanly and spiritually, was one of the greatest gifts of my illness and hospitalization. Every day offered me countless opportunities to receive and offer healing and love. Each one of these that I accepted brought me a deeper experience of God's presence and spirit within and everywhere around me.

The spark of holiness is present in every relationship. We will see it if we are open and willing to let it be revealed to us (T. p. 332; T-17.III.7). As we choose to let each relationship, each encounter we have with another, serve the purpose of reawakening us to the love and holiness that we are, the effects of this healing extend far beyond the particular relationship or encounter.

The Web of Interconnectedness

While I was in the hospital, breakfast was often a very peaceful and reflective time of the day for me. The early morning flurry of hospital routines would be over, and it was generally too early for the phone to start to ring. I would give thanks for the new day and for the food I was about to eat and be very aware of Spirit's presence in my life. Unlike in the usual routine of my life, I was not caught up in things that had to be done that day, and so I was very present in and conscious of *now*, of the present moment.

One morning as I was saying grace, I suddenly became very aware of the extraordinary number of people who had been in some way or other involved in that food ending up on my tray — the farmers who had grown the grain and fruit, the people in factories who had processed and packaged the food, the truckers and railroad workers who had transported it, the distributors who had sold it, the food service workers in the hospital who had prepared the tray and brought it to my bedside.

This sudden awareness deepened in me a precious sense of how interconnected and interdependent we are, with and upon one another. No one of us lives in isolation. We are all profoundly connected and gifted and served by other people, in every aspect of our living. And we are, each one of us, very much a part of that web of service and life.

I saw that, even on this most mundane level, gratitude is due our brothers and sisters — and ourselves — for each of us has a place in the interconnected whole of life. The lives that do not touch our own directly touch other lives that touch yet other lives that somewhere touch lives that touch our own. We are all joined, even when the connection is far beyond the level of our conscious awareness and recognition.

This recognition, which occurred in an instant, filled me with a deep sense of gratitude, as well as a heightened awareness of the reach of my own impact on others. This awareness then unfolded in my experience in a number of ways.

The Shared Nature of Healing

"... our function is to let our minds be healed, that we may carry healing to the world, exchanging curse for blessing, pain for joy, and separation for the peace of God."
                                        — W. pp. 255–56; W-Pt.I.137.13:1

"A miracle is never lost. It may touch many people you have not even met, and produce undreamed of changes in situations of which you are not even aware."
                                        — T. p. 4; T-1.I.45:1–2

I have already shared that one of the major experiences of healing that occurred during my hospital stay was the healing of my relationship with the nursing staff. The shift in my initial perception of the staff as "them," separate and different from "us" (the patients), to a recognition of the staff as human beings, just like me, was a miracle and resulted in many lovely and loving interactions.

After my "breakfast revelation," I became especially aware of how the healing of my relationship with the staff was also reaching beyond our personal interactions. On a very simple and practical level, I began to notice that, when a staff member came into the room flustered or impatient and I would joke or sympathize with them, their mood and manner would often ease and lighten up. As they went on to the next patient, they offered this lightness and good humor instead of the harshness of impatience and frustration.

Like a chain reaction, this would then affect that patient's interaction with the next person who called on the phone, who would then, in turn, carry some effect of that conversation into their next interaction with someone else, and so on. Each offering of kindness and peace increased the likelihood of peace and kindness being further extended.

Because of our interconnectedness, what we offer to others in our encounters with them reaches out in ripple effect far beyond the range of our limited awareness. Each offering of love we make to anyone is magnified and multiplied in scope far beyond what we can even imagine.

"... as you let yourself be healed, you see all those around you, or who cross your mind, or whom you touch or those who seem to have no con-

tact with you, healed along with you. Perhaps you will not recognize them all, nor realize how great your offering to all the world, when you let healing come to you. But you are never healed alone. And legions upon legions will receive the gift that you receive when you are healed."

— W. p. 255; W-Pt.I.137.10

The Course teaches that we are joined at the level of mind — beyond any seeming limitations of physical space or time. Because of this, love extends not only to and through those we directly interact with, but also those we think about — and even beyond, to many more whose specific connection with us only the Holy Spirit within our minds knows.

The more aware I became of this state of deep connectedness, the more I recognized the importance and value of the choice that was mine to make in each moment — the choice to offer love, healing, and peace or to offer judgment, separation, and fear. And I began to experience what I can only describe as a feeling of God's gratitude to me when I would make the loving choice — a feeling so rich and full and beautiful it would inevitably move me to tears. I remembered one of my favorite passages from the Course:

"The Love of God is in everything He created, for His Son is everywhere. Look with peace upon your brothers, and God will come rushing into your heart in gratitude for your gift to Him."

— T. p. 177; T-10.V.7:6–7

The Far Reach of Healing

"When I am healed, I am not healed alone.
And I would share my healing with the world. . . . "

— W. p. 256; W-Pt.I.137.14:3–4

During and shortly after my time in the hospital, several people shared with me powerful experiences of healing in their own lives that were indirectly prompted by the circumstance of my illness and hospitalization. I was very moved by these stories, which also served to further confirm for me the shared nature of our healing.

One of these involved a woman who is a friend and participant in my Course study group. She had become very frightened and upset when she learned that I was in the hospital. Despite the fact that she feels very uncomfortable and nervous in hospitals, she made arrangements to come with another friend to visit me. I was touched by how loving this choice was — the visit itself was an expression of love for me, and allowing herself the support of a friend in a situation that was difficult for her was an expression of love for herself.

During the visit we were all able to laugh gently about the way she handled her discomfort, which was to immediately start making lists for me — thank-you notes I needed to write, things I needed for people to bring me, tasks that needed to be done in my apartment while I was gone....

At the end of the visit, she told me that a healing had occurred for her as an indirect result of her upset about my illness. She shared that she had been praying for a healing in her relationship with her father, who had died about two years before. She had specifically been asking to have a loving memory of him to keep in her heart, something that she felt she did not have.

After finding out about my illness, feeling very upset and realizing how uncomfortable she was with the thought of visiting me in the hospital, she suddenly remembered that her father had been a man who would drop everything and go sit for hours at someone's hospital bedside, simply as an act of human concern and love.

As she remembered this expression of his love for people, she also began to see other things about him in a different light. Certain things that she had judged harshly she could now see for the love they contained and expressed.

Her prayer had been answered. She had received a miracle. And in sharing the story with me, in sharing the love she was now experiencing, she gifted me as well.

The Many Forms of Love

*"The opportunity to respond with love
visits us throughout the day."*

— Karen Casey

The Holy Spirit reaches out to other people through us and to us through other people. The forms in which love can be expressed are myriad — practical help, a word of comfort or understanding, shared laughter, a hand to hold, a prayer offered, a phone call, a listening ear, a book to read, flowers, a note or card, a smile — but the love itself is one.

The chance to offer and receive love is with us throughout our days, wherever we are, whomever we're with. Sometimes these opportunities may surprise us or show themselves in unexpected ways. More than once during my time in the hospital, people came to visit who were ready for and open to a healing in themselves. The Holy Spirit within us brought us together in a time and way that allowed us to share love, to both give and receive the blessings of healing.

This entire experience in my life was a gift of enormous love. Over the months following the hospitalization, people would ask if I was feeling "back to myself." I could only answer that I felt somehow *more* myself — more in touch with and able to express my deeper nature, my real self — than before the experience happened. And for that gift I remain very grateful and feel richly blessed.

I can only say thank you from my heart to everyone who was in any way part of this experience, known or unknown to me, thank you for all the prayers and blessings and healing thoughts, for all the love offered and received, for all the opportunities to feel God's hand at work and presence everywhere. I give thanks for the chance to discover the living truth that, indeed, Love always answers.

So I can only end where I began:

"It's all about love — tell everybody."

References

A Course in Miracles. Glen Ellen, Calif.: Foundation for Inner Peace, 1975, 1992.

The Song of Prayer: Prayer, Forgiveness, Healing: An Extension of the Principles of A Course in Miracles. Glen Ellen, Calif.: Foundation for Inner Peace, 1976, 1992.

Goldsmith, Joel S. *Gift of Love.* New York: HarperCollins, 1993 (1975).

Goldstein, Joseph, and Jack Kornfield. *Seeking the Heart of Wisdom: The Path of Insight Meditation.* Boston: Shambhala Publications, 1987.

Jampolsky, Gerald. *Teach Only Love.* New York: Bantam Books, 1983.

Kornfield, Jack. *A Path with Heart: A Guide through the Perils and Promises of Spiritual Life.* New York: Bantam Books, 1993.

Mitchell, Stephen. *The Gospel According to Jesus.* New York: HarperCollins, 1992.

Morgan, Sheila. "The Divine Dance in Our Daily Life," in *Fellowship in Prayer* (Princeton, N.J.), October 1993.

Nouwen, Henri J. M. *Life of the Beloved.* New York: Crossroad, 1992.

Ram Dass and Paul Gorman. *How Can I Help?* New York: Alfred A. Knopf, 1993 (1985).

Shucman, Helen. *The Gifts of God.* Glen Ellen, Calif.: The Foundation for Inner Peace, 1982.

Skutch, Robert. *Journey without Distance.* Berkeley, Calif.: Celestial Arts, 1984.

Wapnick, Kenneth. *Absence from Felicity: The Story of Helen Shucman and Her Scribing of A Course in Miracles.* Roscoe, N.Y.: Foundation for "A Course in Miracles," 1991.

———. *A Talk Given on A Course in Miracles: An Introduction.* Roscoe, N.Y.: Foundation for "A Course in Miracles," 1989 (1983, 1987).

Wiederkehr, Macrina. *Seasons of Your Heart: Prayers and Reflections*. New York: HarperCollins, 1991.

Additional Information

On Course, a biweekly inspirational magazine published and edited by Jon Mundy and Diane Berke, is available through Interfaith Fellowship. For a sample copy or subscription information, contact: Interfaith Fellowship, 459 Carol Drive, Monroe, NY 10950; (800) 275-4809.

Donna Cary's music tapes — *Real Love, Home Sweet Home, Wake Up*, and *No Solid Ground* — can be ordered through Interfaith Fellowship, or by contacting: Donna Marie Cary, P.O. Box 358, Owensboro, KY 42302.

John Astin's music tapes — *Into the Light, The Winds of Grace, Wake to the Beauty*, and *Remembrance* — can be ordered through Interfaith Fellowship, or by contacting: John Astin, P.O. Box 426, Santa Cruz, CA 95061.

A full listing of books and lecture tapes by Dr. Kenneth Wapnick, as well as a current schedule of workshop offerings, can be obtained by contacting: The Foundation for "A Course in Miracles," R.R. 2, Box 71, Roscoe, NY 12776; (607) 498-4116.

About the Author...

Diane Berke is, together with Jon Mundy, cofounder and senior minister of *Interfaith Fellowship*, an alternative interfaith community of worship in New York City. They also publish the popular biweekly inspirational magazine *On Course*. Diane has a private counseling practice in New York City and has taught in the field of personal and spiritual development for nearly fifteen years. She has been a faculty member and dean of training for the New Seminary, which trains and ordains interfaith ministers. For the last five years she has led classes and workshops on *A Course in Miracles* in the New York area and nationwide.